# THE RELUCTANT EXPAT

## Part Four: Settling Down

## ALAN LAYCOCK

# 1

"So, love, I thought you might like to start doing a bit on the allotment now."

"You did, did you?" Cathy said, her sharp blue eyes X-raying the depths of Bernie's optimistic brain.

He waved his turkey-laden fork and cleared his throat. "Yes, my… our field will be my priority for a while now, so I hoped you might be able to find the time to weed a bit and generally keep an eye on things."

"Ah," she said, before smiling at Inma, who smiled back.

"Yes, I mean, most of my farming mates' wives tend to… er, tend to the veg and whatnot."

"I see," she hissed, a bit like Pol Pot on being told that his breakfast toast had been burnt. "What do you think, Alan?"

"I… well," I began, but before I go on with our Christmas lunch chatter I'd better remind you where we were up to when I signed off at the end of the penultimate part of my *humilem opus*, if that really is how you say 'humble work' in Latin.

The hotel-to-be deal had finally been sealed a couple of weeks earlier and Malcolm and Angela had flown back to Norfolk happy in the knowledge that their right-hand man, namely me, would ensure that Cristóbal finished the job by the end of April, on pain of possibly pain – financial and possibly physical – if he failed to do so. Arturo and Diego had already performed some interior destruction work, so as soon as Cristóbal had seen in the New Year he'd be out there with a platoon of workmen and masses of machinery, or so I hoped. There were many more things going on, of course, but I'll come to them in due course and will now get back to answering Cathy.

"I... well, I plan to cycle over here at least once a week to do some weeding."

"Like you haven't been doing for a while."

"I've been busy."

"You'll be busier now, and so will I, because as well as seeing Doña Elena and Mari Carmen (the oldies she visited) I'm going to do some courses."

"What kind of courses?" Inma asked her in English.

"Oh, I'll see which adult courses are on offer in town. I want to get out and meet some younger local people, you see, as I'm not planning on becoming a... er, *viuda de tractorista*," she said, meaning a tractor driver's widow.

"You can have a go on the tractor if you like," Bernie said with a winning smile, not having grasped the widow bit.

"How thrilling," she murmured.

"When will this field actually become yours, Bern?" I said.

"As soon as I hand over the five and a half grand and we do the paperwork."

"I thought you weren't prepared to pay a cent more than five."

He stabbed a sprout. "I wasn't, but Spartacus is chewing at the bit now, so I've had to meet the old skinflint half way."

"Who is Spartacus?" Inma asked.

"My tractor."

"When did you decide on that name?" Cathy asked.

"This morning on the loo. It suddenly came to me as I was... on the loo. Spartacus started life as a slave, like my tractor, but then gained his freedom and went on to greater things. I've done my research, you see."

"He means he's seen the film," Cathy said.

"What colour will he be?" I asked, as he'd threatened to paint her light-blue to match Letizia, his trusty 2CV.

"Oh, I've decided to stick to the original red. Letizia's a plaything really, but Spartacus will be a serious workhorse and I don't want my farmer pals to laugh at him."

"More turkey?" said Cathy.

"Not for me, thanks," said Inma, unaccustomed as she was to a big Christmas Day feed. The Spaniards usually have a family dinner on Christmas Eve and some go to church on Christmas Day, but the kids aren't supposed to get their presents until *El Día de Los Reyes* – the Day of the Kings – on January 6th, the twelfth day of Christmas, although commercial pressure has ensured that they usually receive a few on Christmas Day too, as it's a bit of a drag getting all their gifts on the day before they go back to school after pining for them for a fortnight. So, Inma and I had decided on an English Christmas, a quiet New Year's Eve, and a Spanish *Reyes* with her parents and other family in Murcia, where the capricious Natalia was sure to make things interesting.

For Christmas I'd bought Bernie a pair of tractor-driving gloves, really standard driving gloves onto the backs of which Inma had skilfully embroidered two little tractors. I'd got Cathy an exciting new Spanish grammar book and a couple of parallel text (Spanish-English) novels, to encourage her to keep up the sterling linguistic work she'd been doing ever since beginning to see her first oldie. They'd given Inma a stylish compact umbrella and me a nifty leather document case which Bernie proposed I carry with me on my site inspections to give me an aura of importance. Inma and I would exchange small gifts on the sixth, we'd agreed, in keeping with tradition.

After lunch Bernie and I strolled down to the impeccable but lacklustre allotment and he pointed out the potatoes, onions and garlic which he hoped to harvest within a month or two.

"Ah, good. Oh, what happened to all the other things we planted?" I asked, as apart from some beans and carrots I'd seen few fruits of our labours.

"Well, I think we started a bit late. Only the radishes did really well." He shrugged. "Pity no-one likes them."

"Hmm, are you serious about expecting Cathy to lend a hand? She does look after the non-edibles, after all."

"I know, but remember the dog scare we've just had," he said, referring to the possible adoption of an unwanted terrier called Luna which Cathy's friend Denise had finally placed with a local family whose younger members had drooled over the poor little thing. "I don't want a dog really, as they tie you down so much, so I'd like Cathy to keep busy."

"Won't the field and this tie you down?" I said, pointing to the largely fallow plot.

"Not as much. I'd like us to take a few trips this year and I will *not* have a puppy peeing in Letizia. We still haven't seen much of Spain."

"No, me neither. Hopefully when the hotel's up and running Inma and me will get away too. I want to have a look up north, as it's said to be like a different country."

"Yes, me too. How's your pal Zeferino, by the way?"

"Rejuvenated since resuming his swimming and popping up to his country pad every week."

"Does the old buffer not get under your feet?"

"Not at all. Him and our neighbour are as thick as thieves now. He's agreed to house-sit while we're in Murcia, from his command post in the annex, and he's sure to spend most of his time with Álvaro. They'll regale each other with further tall historical tales, which will be a big improvement on all the solitary holidays they must have spent in the past."

"That's true."

"Oh, how's Jesús?" I said, having forgotten to ask after my ailing pal and sometime employer who Bernie now assisted gratis once or twice a week.

"He's finished his treatment and the doctors are optimistic, but he does like to harp on about the Big C. The other day in his casita he told me to examine my bollocks."

"What, there?"

"No, at home. Although he's got prostate cancer, he's fond of quoting statistics about the other types too. It seems to have become something of an obsession with him."

"Yes, I know. Juan told me that when he enters Vicente's bar everyone starts fidgeting and trying to get out of the way, as he's sure to prod them somewhere or other and tell them what their chances of survival are. Juan says they're awaiting the day when he gets the all-clear so they can stop being sympathetic and tell him to put a lid on it."

"Hmm, and the stronger he gets, the less tractor driving I'm allowed to do. Still, I'm glad he's getting better and I'll soon have my own field to plough."

"Will… er, Spartacus be able to handle that hard earth and mass of weeds?"

"No."

"No?"

"No, a mate of mine will give it a going over with his super-duper tractor first, as I don't want to strain Spartacus and the old plough I'll soon be buying."

"Will you plant almond trees like you said then?"

"No, olive trees."

"Oh, right. Why have you changed your mind?"

"Because there's a boom in planting almond trees right now."

"So?"

He scratched his tanned, freshly shaven head and smiled. "They've been planting almond trees like mad in Spain for the last couple of years, as prices have been high, so I'm going to buck the trend and plant olive trees. Five years from now when they start to bear fruit I'll be quids in, you'll see."

"And what do your grizzled *agricultor* mates say about that?"

"Ha, they think I'm wrong and try to persuade me to plant almond trees or even vines, but because I'm foreign they have an inkling that I might know something they don't, so they're a bit intrigued really."

"Why should you know something they don't just because you're foreign?"

"Oh, well, they aren't the most cultured men in the world and as most agricultural innovations have come from abroad they don't quite know what to make of me. I like to seem a bit enigmatic anyway, so that they don't take me for a complete wally."

"I bet you do. Come on, it's getting chilly."

"Hmm, but it's not much of a winter here, is it?"

"Inma says winter really starts in January."

"Yes, my mates do too, but we're used to real winters."

"Yes, and central heating. Have you got enough firewood?"

"Oh, yes, what's left of the ton we bought will see us out, no problem. Sold any coins lately?" he asked as we wandered past the covered pool.

"No. What with all the excitement over the hotel project I haven't done a thing."

"You ought to keep your eye in though."

"I know."

"Why not invest in some really good coins now that you're rolling in it?"

I pictured the cornflakes box full of cash in the pantry. "Yes, I suppose I could do that, then keep them for a rainy day. Good idea, Bern."

He shrugged before skipping up the porch steps and turning to face me. "But if you play your cards right there might not be any rainy days for the foreseeable. Once the hotel's finished, Angela's planning to keep you gainfully employed, isn't she?"

"Yes, but as what? And what if things don't go to plan and Malcolm chews me up and sprays my remains all over his wife's unfinished project?"

He laughed. "Ah, good old Alan, always the optimist. Come on, I fancy a drop of that new brandy."

"Me too," I said, my new executive responsibilities having already made me turn to drink – a glass of wine almost every day for the last few weeks.

# 2

"Let's have a drink first," said Cristóbal on the second of January when I met him in the still lamplit town, prior to driving over to the hotel project to meet his crack building team. It was a cold, damp morning and I felt a great sense of anticipation, marred only slightly by anxiety.

"We'll go to Vicente's bar, as Arturo and Diego might be there."

"All right. That gypsy pal of yours seems to be a good worker after all, and I don't think he's nicked anything yet."

"He isn't a gypsy... or a thief," I said, almost sure that he'd put his wayward ways behind him since he'd started seeing more of his young daughter Rocío.

"Well, I just hope he's as good at building things as he is at pulling them down. Him and Diego have demolished nearly all the partition walls that had to go, so we've now got an almost blank canvas to work on," he said in his usual gruff manner as we shot up the narrow street in his van.

"Yes, that was a good idea of mine."

He grunted approvingly and screeched to a halt outside the bar.

"What are you doing here at this time?" I asked Jesús at the bar, as it was just after seven and would be dark for at least another hour.

"I know it's late for me to be here, but since my illness I've been taking things easy. Vicente, get these boys whatever they want."

I ordered a *cortado* and Cristóbal a *café solo* and a glass of Soberano brandy.

"Are you still in pain?" I asked Jesús on seeing him wince.

He nodded at the brandy glass, him not being a big spender. "No, I'm feeling much better now."

"Yes, you look like your old self again."

He raised a forefinger and stared at me. "Alan, I'll *never* be the same again, not after my cancer, which might still return."

I noticed Vicente wringing a dry dishcloth and staring up at the ceiling, except that his eyes were scrunched shut. A short, elderly man called Ernesto took two steps to the left, sliding his cup and saucer with him. Jesús observed Cristóbal pouring a little brandy into his coffee.

"Cristóbal, have you checked your balls lately?"

He sputtered. "You what?"

Vicente coughed lightly. "Jesús is on testicular cancer this week. It was lung cancer before that."

By way of reply, Cristóbal took a packet of fags from his shirt pocket and slapped it onto the bar.

Jesús shook his head sadly. "I've just given up, though I didn't smoke much anyway. Did you know that of the seven men here now–"

"Shut up, Jesús!" Vicente barked more sternly than I'd heard him speak, or bark, before. "Cristóbal hasn't been here for ages and your bloody obsession is going to drive him away."

"I paid for his drinks," he mumbled.

"You're ca... illness is becoming bad for trade," he snapped, seeming genuinely annoyed.

"People should be prepared for the worst."

"Well prepare them for it somewhere else. Another word about... that and I'll bar you, and I mean it."

"What are you doing on the land now, Jesús?" I interjected, expecting quite enough stress later on at the house.

"Pruning some of the trees, and ploughing, of course. Bernie has been a great help."

"I'm glad."

"Yes, *he* really does have a feel for the land, though it's foolish of him to want to plant olive trees now."

I sniggered enigmatically, or tried to. "Hmm, maybe Bernie knows something you lot don't," I said, and as Cristóbal had supped up right on cue, I left him to mull that one over.

"No Diego or Arturo," Cristóbal said in the van.

"They'll be there already, I expect. The sun never rises quickly enough for those two."


As we approached the country house the sky was lightening to the east – as it usually does – and Arturo's old van was the only vehicle to be seen on the gravelled area to the side of the long, graceful, two-storey building whose innards were about to be transformed.

"Where are the others?" I asked.

"They'll be here at eight, or they'd better be."

"And the building materials?"

"They'll be here at nine, or they'd better be."

"It's a big job, isn't it?" I said as we stepped out of the van.

"Yes, but it's become a bit simpler since last night."

"Oh?"

"Did you not see the email that Malcolm sent at about half nine?"

"Not yet, no. What did he say?"

"Oh, not much really, only that they no longer want to have their own quarters in the hotel."

I gazed at the fading moon and almost howled. "What? But that's an intrinsic part of the plans."

"Yes, it was, but I must say the updated ones are very good. The hotel will now have three more bedrooms, with en suite bathrooms, of course. It'll make things simpler for me, but no cheaper for him, as I've already pointed out."

"But where will they stay?"

"I couldn't care less, unless he intends to build another house, in which case I'll care very much, as I'll be building it." He took out his phone and swiped it. "Here it is."

I saw that Malcolm, as was usual in his curt missives, had written no more than was strictly necessary.

"Well that's a surprise," I said as I handed back the phone.

"It might be good news for you, if you do end up working here. Nothing worse than having the boss breathing down your neck."

"But I can't see Angela wanting to be too far away. Anyway, I'll speak to her soon. Here are two more vans."

"My lads with all our gear. The new blokes had better be here in ten minutes as I don't want to start the day with a bollocking."

"Where are they from?" I said as we strolled towards the house.

"You'll see."

"Foreigners?"

"You'll see." He pushed the main door and found it locked. "Where have those two got to?"

"Al-an! Cristó-bal!" Arturo cried as they approached from the direction of the swimming pool which the caretaker was still keeping clean, now at Malcolm and Angela's expense. Diego was swinging a flask which I hoped contained their morning coffee.

"Hola," he grunted, looking far less chirpy than his sidekick, although Arturo had assured me that he hadn't touched a drop on the job, him being my eyes and ears on site unless I was there, in which case I'd use my own.

Cristóbal's regular crew of four skilled builders trooped over and uttered muted greetings, after which we stood there on the tiled patio, looking expectantly down the drive.

At eight o'clock on the dot Cristóbal clapped his hands. "Right, bring in the gear and we'll make a start."

"What about the new blokes?" said Miguel, a cheerless man of forty and nothing at all like that other Miguel, Natalia's ex-boyfriend, who still popped up in my dreams from time to time, though Natalia had assured her mother that he was now a mere footnote in history and no longer even worked at the university refectory.

"What about them? Do you want me to organise a little dance so that you can get to know them?"

"No, Cristóbal," he muttered.

"I'll lead the dance," said Arturo, twirling around and twisting his hands in the air, before clapping and stamping his feet.

To my surprise, Cristóbal actually smiled, as did Diego, while the others looked on grimly, as Arturo hadn't yet had the opportunity to work his magic on them.

Just then a noisy blue van trundled up the drive, juddered to a halt, and five men aged between about thirty and sixty piled out, stretching and yawning, before each pulled out a large rucksack or travel bag. Cristóbal strode over with me hot on his heels.

"Cristóbal?" the oldest and smallest man asked, the others all being strapping chaps.

He grunted and surveyed his imported team who were undoubtedly Spanish. As it was ten past eight I thought he might berate them, but he merely asked the man how their journey had been.

"Not bad. We set off at five, but we're ready to go. I'm Rafael," he said, offering his hand to Cristóbal.

After shaking he found mine poised, as I was keen to avail them of my key role right away.

"I'm Alan. I'm here on behalf of the owners."

"Encantado, Alan," said the bald, wiry chap who looked a bit like a more rugged version of Bernie.

"Where have you come from?"

"From Tomelloso and nearby, in Castilla-La Mancha."

"Oh, right, that's a long way from here."

"About 250 kilometres by the fastest route," he said in a clear, pleasant voice.

"Oh, will you drive there–"

"Right, enough chatter," Cristóbal interrupted. "Come on, I'll show you your rooms."

"Rooms?" I said, but the rude blighter had already marched off, so I followed them into the house.

It transpired that the Manchegos, as they soon became known, were to stay at the house during the week, initially in two of the bedrooms which had survived Arturo and Diego's sledgehammering. To my surprise I saw five tatty mattresses piled up in one of them and I murmured to Cristóbal that it had been thoughtful of him to provide them.

"They'll need them after eleven or twelve hours' work," he muttered.

"Does, er, Malcolm know they're staying here?"

He glared at me. "It's nothing to do with him. While the work's going on, this place is effectively mine," he said, helpfully pointing at his formidable chest.

"All right."

"What's in that?"

I held up the document case. "Er, a notepad, and pens."

"What for?"

"To make notes. I have to feedback to our employers, remember."

He grunted. "The best thing you can do is stay out of our way."

I raised myself to my full height of six foot one and glowered down, though I still felt somehow smaller than him. "Think yourself lucky that I didn't *oblige* you to employ *me* on this job, from beginning to end," I growled.

He prodded me lightly just under the ribcage. "I have a watertight con-tract, Alan, and you're not mentioned in it, so behave yourself," he said with a sneer.

It then occurred to me to make a joke which turned out unexpectedly well.

"Ha, before long I'll be pulling the…er, building strings in this area, so *you* behave yourself, Cristóbal."

Bernie's talk of being enigmatic in the presence of his farming pals had inspired me to say that, and instead of laughing in my face, Cristóbal raised his eyebrows and pouted thoughtfully. He wasn't one for pouting much, generally speaking, so I underlined my absurd point by slapping my case, clicking my tongue and heading purposefully for the door, before stomping from room to room, making copious and mainly meaningless notes. When I returned ten minutes later, casually displaying a page covered in aggressive handwriting, Rafael had moved into another room with his youngest colleague, who turned out to be his son, while the other three had laid down their mattresses in the first room and unloaded cooking equipment and other sundry items.

I heard Cristóbal barking instructions to his regular crew downstairs, so I asked Rafael and his son, a stocky chap called David (with the stress on the i) how they'd ended up working on this distant job.

"Oh, we often work away from home, usually on the coast," said Rafael. "I don't quite know how Cristóbal located me, but we'd just finished a big job in Benidorm, so I agreed to come here for six weeks."

"Only six weeks?"

"Yes, that's what he said. I think he intends to get all the main work done in that time, then let his boys finish things off." He shrugged and smiled. "It suits me to have a definite end date, so that I can line something up for later, probably on the coast again."

"I see. Do you never work close to home?"

"Oh, before the crisis we did for a few years, but I sensed that a slump was coming, so we still kept doing jobs on the coast from time to time."

"And after the crisis?"

"Things were quiet, but we did better than most."

"Papá has always kept us in work," David said proudly.

"It must be hard to be away from home every week," I said.

"Oh, one gets used to it," said Rafael. "Often on the coast we'd only go home every other weekend."

"Twelve days working twelve hours a day," said his son. "A lot of work and a lot of money."

"Is Cristóbal… is this contract to your satisfaction?"

"Yes, it's fine. I told your friend our rates and he agreed," said Rafael. He clapped and rubbed his rough hands together. "Only four days this week, then home for Reyes, so we'd better get started."

"Yes, er… if there's ever anything you're not happy about, please have a word with me," I said, fluttering my pad and gazing into his eyes enigmatically.

"Sure, Alan. Come on, son, let's show these Alicantinos how to work."

Left alone in the makeshift bedroom I gazed out of the window at the pool and the fields beyond and felt a spell of profound thinking coming on, so I pulled up a chair and sat down in order to allow the blood to reach my brain more easily. As I listened to the voices, thuds and scraping sounds below, I found myself smiling and stretching languorously. Having already seen Cristóbal's crew at work I knew they were capable, hard-working men, and I felt sure that the Manchegos would be every bit as good as them. At that moment I had no doubts at all that the work would be finished by the end of April, if not before, as with twelve men going at it hammer and tongue for six weeks they'd get an awful lot done.

Cristóbal didn't only give orders, you see, but also led by example on most jobs, so the nine, no, twelve-bedroom hotel would gradually take shape before my observant eyes and I'd be able to reassure Angela that her dream project was progressing smoothly. Malcolm would be pleased with my masterful management and who knew what the future might hold? Maybe they'd decide to build a house nearby and ask me to oversee proceedings, and as I looked out over my domain I imagined all sorts of edifices. A conservatory, a greenhouse, a café and even a bandstand popped up all over the place, and Malcolm might also require his own golf course, and who better than I to find the location and even design the course, playfully placing bunkers here and there and creating picturesque ponds for him to chip his balls over?

The fact that I knew nothing at all about building or landscaping seemed irrelevant and I'd just decided to take a tour of the grounds with my trusty document case when I heard raised voices from below. I sighed, stood up, and endeavoured to maintain my dreamlike serenity as I descended the stairs, where I found Arturo and the biggest of the Manchegos apparently on the point of coming to blows in the lobby, while the others looked on. There was no sign of Cristóbal.

I approached with my document case enfolded in my arms and came to a halt at the spot where a boxing referee would have stood. Arturo had adopted a pugilistic stance, while the Manchego stood with his hands on his hips, possibly planning to swat away the much smaller man should he dare to unleash a blow. At that critical moment I found it expedient to imagine Bernie standing across from me, observing how I handled this tricky business.

"What's going on?" I asked calmly.

"This big oaf is a racist swine," Arturo whined without dropping his guard.

"It was a joke," said the hefty, swarthy chap of about forty.

"He asked what a bloody *gitanillo* was doing on site, and though I'm not a gypsy, I might have been. Is that any way to behave in this day and age, Alan?"

"It was just a joke, man. With your hair and those rings I thought you must be one of us."

"These rings come off when I start work and... what do you mean, one of us?"

The man chuckled gutturally and let his arms fall by his side. "I'm quarter gypsy and proud of it. I was just joking, I tell you."

"Quarter gypsy?" Arturo said, scratching his temple with his fist.

"My grandmother, may she rest in peace. And you?"

"Half gypsy, my father."

"Really?" said the referee.

"Yes, Alan. Look, with gypsies I'm a gypsy and with payos I'm a payo. (Payo is the word that gypsies use for everybody else.) It makes life easier. All right, man, you were joking," he said, offering his hand, which the quarter gypsy shook.

"Where's Cristóbal?" I asked.

"Gone to town for something," said one of his men.

"Fortunately," said another.

"As he doesn't like gypsies," said the first.

"What?" said the quarter gypsy.

"He *thinks* he doesn't like gypsies," said Arturo with a chuckle. "But I'm educating him. He's all right really."

"It might be best if we don't mention this little… incident," I said.

"I'm sure we'll all get on fine," said Rafael, who would probably have stepped in if I hadn't appeared. "I only hope that you boys can keep up with us."

"Ha," said Diego. "We'll show you Manchegos how to work."

As almost every word I'd spoken that day seemed to have hit the spot, I ventured the following witticism.

"Ha, since I've lived here I've seen that Alicantinos are the laziest workers in the country, if not the world, so I'm sure you Manchegos will work much faster."

With twelve local eyes glaring at me I pointed out that it was a joke.

"Pah, some joke," said Diego, and on hearing the sound of wheels on gravel they all sprang into action, leaving me to rue my silly jest after so successfully diffusing that sticky situation.

As you'll have already gathered, I do have a tendency to enter a fantasy world from time to time, but that slight clanger brought me back down to earth and I did go to tour the grounds, not to plan preposterous structures, but to stay out of the way and let them get on with it. A lorry soon arrived with a huge load of sand and a van brought dozens of bags of cement and other materials, but as this book isn't a building or any other kind of manual I'll be sparing you most of the details regarding the ins and outs of the construction work. Human interaction is what interests me, though by midday I'd seen that little enough of that appeared to be on the cards, as Cristóbal had the Manchegos and Alicantinos working in separate teams. Cristóbal's squad, though good workers, were a dull lot on the whole, apart from Arturo, and the Manchegos seemed no more forthcoming, except Rafael, who usually had something to say when I passed by with my document case, unlike Cristóbal, who studiously ignored me until about one o'clock.

"I'm off for lunch now," he said as he walked past with a pneumatic drill on his shoulder.

"Oh, I'd better come with you," I said, having slipped no sandwiches into my handy case.

"Of course. If you've seen enough for today, I'll drop you in town."

"All right."

As we sped along in the van I expressed my optimism regarding the timely outcome of the work.

"Of course, I told you I had everything under control."

Liar, I thought, as he'd been panicking about not finding enough workers, and even feared having to employ nasty foreigners.

"How did you find the Manchegos?"

"Oh, through contacts. They have a good reputation, but aren't cheap."

"I hope they'll be comfortable there."

He shrugged. "They're used to sleeping on site and they have plenty of room. They can use the kitchen until we start to renovate it, and there are plenty of chairs and things around the place."

"They might be a bit cold," I said, as night-time temperatures had already dipped below freezing a few times.

"I'll take a couple of gas heaters after lunch. Don't worry about them or anything else, Alan. The job is big but straightforward. You don't even have to go if you have anything better to do."

"I'll go twice a week, as I told Angela I would."

He shrugged. "As you wish. Oh, when you speak to her, ask her where they plan to live." He released the wheel and rubbed his hands together. "I think a nice three-bedroom chalet with a private pool would be best, over to the right of the house, eh?"

"I'll ask her."

"Persuade her."

"I'll ask her."

"Five percent for you, Alan."

"We'll see. They might have other plans."

"I can see no alternative if she wishes to be near her *hotelito*."

I sighed with relief when he slowed to 50kph in the urban zone, as he was a truly demonic driver.

"Drop me here. I'll drive over on Friday morning."

"OK. Speak to Angela and find out when they're coming, and... you know."

"Yes, I know."


By the time Inma arrived home from the bar at seven I'd spoken to Angela and also bought a 1658 Oliver Cromwell silver shilling at the bargain price of £1,499, plus registered post to Spain.

"Isn't that a lot of money for an old coin, Alan?"

"Not for this one. I'd have called to ask your permission to buy it, but it was such a bargain that I couldn't risk losing it. It had only been on sale for a few hours and I know the seller and he must need to free up some cash, as the coin's easily worth two thousand or more," I babbled.

She chuckled and grasped my cheek between finger and thumb, something I think she'd seen Cathy do. "Ask my permission? Why, it's your money?"

"Our money, and there's too much of it in that cereal box."

"Oh, I forgot about that. Which one is it? I threw one away yesterday."

I made to dash to the larder, but remembered that I'd checked it that afternoon, again.

"I'm joking, silly, but I don't feel comfortable with it in the house either. Why don't you put it in the bank?"

My eyes opened wide. "But it's black money, remember. They might ask me where it came from."

She laughed in that endearing tinkly way of hers. "Oh, Alan, you're so funny sometimes."

"Am I?"

"Yes. I mean, who's to know where the money came from? You're a foreigner, remember, and twenty thousand isn't so much."

"Nearer nineteen now, as I've… withdrawn some money."

"Put most of it in the bank soon, cariño. What did Angela have to say?"

As I poured the tea I told her that I'd reassured my boss that the building team was top notch and that I had every confidence in them.

"And have you?"

"Yes, I think so. I'd expected Cristóbal to pick up stray workers from here and there, but the Manchego boys are a tried and tested squad who've done many bigger jobs than this one."

"What did she say about the new plans?"

"Hmm, it seems that was a snap decision of Malcolm's. He suddenly realised that he wouldn't want to be so near to the guests, so he had his architect come round on Sunday evening and modify the plans. I asked her where they planned to stay when they come over and she told me that Malcolm had come up with an idea, but wouldn't tell her what it was."

"That's strange."

"Apparently he likes to surprise her from time to time, normally with jewels and things, so she's sure it'll be something good."

"So there'll be no new house for Cristóbal to build?"

"It appears not. Not yet, anyway, and I didn't like to pry."

"Did you ask her when they're coming out?"

"Yes, but she wasn't sure. That's also part of Malcolm's surprise, it seems, and I think he also wants to surprise me and Cristóbal, so I don't know when they'll come."

"Malcolm seems to be full of surprises."

I intertwined my fingers and stretched my arms in the air. "Yes, and whenever he comes he's going to be surprised by how much work has been done. With a dozen men under Cristóbal's command they'll transform that place in no time." I sipped my tea and sighed contentedly. "Ah, I really do think this building business is going to go more smoothly than I imagined. I'll call round twice a week, but I'd better start thinking about doing something else too."

Inma looked at the ceiling, so I did too.

"Something wrong with the lamp, dear?"

"No, I'm looking through the ceiling."

"Ah, yes," I said, as I knew she hadn't gone mad or acquired X-ray vision, but was subtly referring to my projected patio project. At midnight on New Year's Eve after we'd each eaten twelve grapes, as is the custom, neither of us had thought about making resolutions, mainly because we were tired out and soon fell into bed, but you may remember that before Christmas I'd resolved to retile Zefe's crummy living room to limber up for the rooftop patio I meant to construct, along with steps up the slope between the house and Zefe's… our annex.

"Yes, I guess there's nothing to stop me putting my new skills into practice now. I think Zefe's in residence from tomorrow, so

I'll take him to buy the tiles and also have a look at some for the patio."

"And the steps."

"And the steps?"

"Yes, we don't want ugly concrete steps, do we? Bring a few samples and have a look at railings too. Are you all right, Alan?"

My head must have drooped due to the increasing weightiness of the job. I mean, making a decent set of steps would test me to the limit, let alone tiling the tricky devils.

"Yes, I'm… hmm, it's a pity that Arturo's tied up now, as he could have… lent me a hand."

She chuckled and ruffled my hair. "Look, tile Zefe's floor, because you did promise to, and then think carefully about the work here. If it's too difficult I'm sure we'll be able to find someone who can… lend you a hand."

I smiled sheepishly. "I'm not a very handy man, am I?"

"But you're willing to learn, and I'm sure you're capable of greater things than building anyway. What's for dinner?"

"Goulash Madrileño."

She raised her hands to her ears. "Oh, don't remind me of that awful little man," she said, referring, of course, to Natalia's ex. "What have you really made?"

"Er, Goulash Alicantino then. His dish did inspire it, I'm afraid."

She wrinkled her cute little nose. "I can't smell it."

"I made it hours ago. It improves with age, I think. Would you like it with rice?"

"Doesn't it have potatoes?"

"Er, not the Alicantino version."

"Oh."

"No, I forgot to put them in."

"Ah. Rice then."

I jumped up and within a minute two packets of microwaveable rice were on the go, such is my idea of culinary excellence. The goulash was rather good though, I must say.

# 3

"Those will do," Zefe said the next morning at the builders' merchant's after I'd intercepted him between the annex and Álvaro's house and bundled him into the car.

"They're the first ones you've seen, Zefe. There are loads more to choose from."

"Bah, who cares? It's only a floor."

"Do you want me to tile it, or not?" I asked, refraining from crossing my fingers behind my back, as the floor was a crumbling eyesore and had to be replaced.

"Yes, but how long will it take you?"

"That I don't know. It'll be my first solo tiling job, so it might take a while. Three days, perhaps."

He raised his sharp brown eyes to meet mine. "What, during the week?"

"That's when work is normally done, yes," I said, but I knew what he was getting at. His usual days in the annex were from Tuesday to Thursday or Wednesday to Friday, as Inma had insisted that he mustn't get used to staying for more than two nights at a time, not because she didn't like him, but because had it been up to him he'd have moved in permanently in order to be near his history buddy. We rarely saw him anyway, and both felt philanthropic about giving the old devil a new lease of life, but it wouldn't do to let him get too used to it, as Natalia would stay there in the holidays and other guests would appear by and by, such as my sister Christine's brood from Canada.

Zefe looked at my watch, as he didn't wear one himself, claiming to be too old to wish to observe the passing of time.

"For heaven's sake, Zefe, you'll be with your beloved Álvaro within the hour."

"Beloved?" he snapped.

"Your good friend, I mean. Look, we'll arrange your visits around the tiling."

"Really?"

"Yes."

"All right then. The two nights you allow me to stay in the country are precious to me, you know. I think they're what are keeping me alive."

"What? Spending hours on end in Álvaro's musty living room?"

"No more than five or six hours a day, Alan. I also sit in my doorway looking out across the countryside, reflecting on my long and varied life."

Yes, and getting through gas bottles like there's no tomorrow, I thought but didn't say.

"Take your time choosing the tiles while I go and look for some for the annex patio," I said.

He beamed. "Ah, yes, a patio above the annex will be lovely, but you mustn't make the steps too steep for my old legs, Alan."

"No, Zefe."

Half an hour later a young assistant helped me to load my old Clio with the beige tiles which Zefe had chosen, plus two big tubs of special mortar and four sample tiles for our patio.

"Gracias," I said to the lad, handing him a €5 note, me being a rich foreigner.

"Muchas gracias. Er, do you already have the *rodapié* to go with the tiles?"

"Ah, yes, the rodapié… yes," I said, stalling for time while I tried to remember what it was, as by then I hated to admit not knowing an essential word, and the lad's tone suggested it was important.

"Oh, we don't need to bother with a rodapié, Alan," said Zefe.

I smiled. "Why not?"

"Well, the old one isn't so different, and only a few bits are loose. You can just stick them back on."

I clicked. Rodapié meant skirting board, or in the case of Zefe's antiquated living room, skirting tiles. I turned to the expectant lad. "Do you have… er, wooden rodapiés?"

"Of course."

I slammed the boot. "Come on, Zefe."

"Oh, Alan, Álvaro will be worri… waiting for me."

"He can wait. You'll be there for a long time anyway, as you're staying over Reyes, remember?"

His face lit up. "Oh, yes, I forgot. I'll need to buy some more food then."

"First the rodapié, then food," I said as the lad looked on, probably wondering how or why the gangly guiri had adopted this trying old man.

After buying cream skirting boards that I hoped would be a little higher than the existing tiles, plus a suitable adhesive, we headed to his flat, where Zefe offered words of encouragement while I made repeated trips up the stairs, first from my car and then from the builders' merchant's delivery van. Once I'd stacked the materials in the corner of the room, I opened his biography of Peter the Great and withdrew several notes.

"I owe you nine euros, Zefe."

"Don't be ridiculous, Alan. It is I who owe you. Oh, and take some money for the gas I'm using."

I slid out a twenty.

"Take a fifty too."

"No…"

"Take it! Why the devil should it *cost* you to have a useless old man staying in your beautiful annex?"

I took a fifty instead of the twenty.

"I worry about you, Alan," he said when I'd slid his current account back into place on the shelf.

"Why's that?"

"You're too soft. I worry that people will exploit your generosity."

"Yes, well, I doubt Inma will allow that to happen."

"That's true. At least she has her head in its place. You must marry her, Alan, while she still loves you."

"We haven't talked about that yet."

"Why not?" he said, before sitting in his armchair and pointing his stick at the other one.

I sat. "Well, neither of us is religious, and we don't feel the need to sign some papers to confirm our… attachment."

"Hmm, but if you live together it's best to be united in the eyes of the law, especially you, Alan, as the house is hers and you might find yourself out on the street one day."

"Ha."

He tutted. "Women can be temperamental creatures, Alan. I should know. Once in… Bolivia I had a young–"

"Oh, no, Zefe." I cried. "Don't start one of your stories after what you've just said."

"All right, but propose to her soon."

"No, Zefe. Due to the fact that the house is hers, as you so subtly pointed out, I'll wait for her to decide if she wants to marry me," I said, surprised to find myself articulating thoughts that I'd scarcely had, at least not in my conscious mind.

"A Spanish woman expects her man to propose to her."

"Yes, well, we'll see about that. It's early days."

"I too must think about tying up some legal loose ends in my life," he said, or words to that effect.

"Oh, what?"

"My will, of course. I was thinking of leaving everything to you, Alan."

I gulped. "Don't be daft, Zefe."

"Daft? Why daft? If I don't my *bastardo* of a son will get everything."

"Er, it's not very nice to call your son a bastard, Zefe."

"No, I suppose not, and we did marry shortly before he was born, but what else should I call a son who is incapable of travelling from Cataluña to see his old father?"

"Neglectful."

"Yes, well, the neglectful bastard isn't getting a single peseta from me. As I say, I was thinking of leaving it all to you, but now I feel I should provide for my friend Álvaro too."

"Yes, you ought to do that," I said, before looking around the brightly painted living room and through the door to the crummy kitchen.

"I'm not a rich man, Alan."

"No."

"But I'm not so poor either. Don't let this place deceive you."

"I won't, but look, I hope you don't think for a minute that I befriended you with any ulterior motive in mind."

"Of course not."

"Good."

"You're far too guileless to think in that way."

"Yes, I am. If you really don't want to leave your son anything, leave it to Álvaro, as I think the money would be helpful to him."

"I know, but he's an old man, Alan."

"He's about fifteen years younger than you."

"True." He sighed. "When I stopped pretending to be ninety-odd and became eighty-four once more I felt younger for a while, but now that I'm eighty-five I feel old again."

"You're in good health. As long as you don't drink too much wine, you'll live for a long time yet."

"I drink less now, as Álvaro drinks little."

"Good, and we'll get back to our swimming after Reyes."

"Ah, yes. You know, I could happily die in the pool."

"Hmm, but it might be unpleasant for the rest of the people in it."

"True. Oh, I hope I don't die in your lovely annex. That could be *very* inconvenient for you."

The morbid turn our conversation had taken disturbed me less than you might imagine, as I could sense that the old rogue was leading up to something wicked, imaginary, or both.

"Why? I'd just have you carted off in an ambulance and think no more of it."

He grinned. "Ah, yes, but when they discover you to be my heir, they'll probably think you murdered me."

I nodded and scratched my head. "Hmm, good point. If you do put me in your will, the temptation will certainly be there. As you say, Inma could throw me out at any time, so once you've made it I'll probably keep you up there and somehow speed your demise. Arsenic might be the thing."

He waved his finger and tutted. "No, no, Alan, far too obvious. The autopsy would incriminate you straight away. You could try using polonium, but no, that too would probably be detected these days. Ha, I know! Have you ever been to the woods to collect wild mushrooms in autumn?"

"Not yet, but I'd like to."

He rubbed his hands together. "Right, well, most edible mushrooms are white, but one can also find a similar one which is white but with a yellow-green hue, a bit like these walls that you painted."

"Hmm, that would be ironic and somehow fitting, yes."

"The poisonous ones are called oronja verde, or sometimes oronja mortal, as they are indeed deadly."

"I'll look them up on the computer."

"You do that. The good thing about mushrooms is that I could have collected them myself."

"Yes, so I'd better wear gloves when I pick them."

He shuffled on his chair. "Yes, be sure to do that. Once when I was logging in the Amazon rainforest, on the Peruvian side, I had a tiresome colleague called Julio César."

"Like the emperor?"

"Yes, and he too had delusions of grandeur and wished to take more than his share of our profits, so one day I set out with my mule and after crossing a raging torrent I..." and he was off, telling me his first tall tale for a while, having forgotten that he was eager to meet up with Álvaro, so I happily heard him out. "... so the autopsy in Lima proved nothing and I kept his earnings too."

"I'm glad. Shall we go now?"

"Yes, we'd better call at the supermarket."

"Oh, there's plenty of food in the cave and Álvaro can fetch bread from town."

On driving up the track I saw that Inma had arrived home early, her and Rosa now having dependable staff, including Randi, who cooked four or five days a week.

"I'll give you a key to the cave when we leave on Friday, Zefe."

"All right, I'll keep an eye on things."

"Thanks."

"Ask Inma to marry you before she gets bored of you, Alan."

"Bye, Zefe."


Of the four sample tiles I'd brought, Inma preferred a thick, reddish one, providing they had smaller ones available for the steps too.

"I forgot to ask, but I'm sure they'll be able to get them."

"I was up on the roof earlier having a look. It would be nice to make the patio sort of curve towards the steps rather than having a gap in between."

"Yes," I said, picturing the nifty tile cutter that I'd only ever used for cutting straight lines, under Arturo's supervision.

She smiled. "Have you seen your friend Juan lately?"

"Not for a while, no. I'll call him soon."

"Is he still doing trips for the furniture company?"

"I don't think he's done any for a while. I expect they'll call him when they need him."

"Hmm, he might be getting bored at home then, or in the bar."

"Yes, he might. What are you getting at, love?"

"Well, he knows a lot about building, doesn't he?"

"Quite a lot, yes."

"Well then, when you get round to doing the patio – and there's no hurry at all – you could ask him to come up to give you a bit of advice." She grasped my not entirely unbeefy bicep. "You've got the muscles to do the job, and if he's got the know-how, you'll have a nice time up there together."

"Brilliant," I cried, grasping her slender arm. "Yes, I bet he'd enjoy that and I would like to see more of him. I haven't been to

Vicente's much because I don't think I'm a bar person," I said, immediately picturing Reggie Perrin's bearded son-in-law in that wonderful series.

"Una persona de bar?" she asked, nonplussed.

"A person who likes going to them."

"Ah."

"I prefer to see people one-to-one, really. I find that the more people there are, the less interesting the conversation tends to be."

"Yes, we might find that's the case at my parents' house on Saturday."

I inhaled sharply. "I'd prefer to meet them quietly one day. Oh, are we not going until Saturday?"

She put her arms around my waist and gazed into my perturbed eyes.

"Yes, I'll spare you Friday night, and we'll come back on Saturday evening."

"Right, so Zefe won't have to look after the house for long," I said, striving to hide my pleasure at the brevity of our visit.

"It'll seem odd if you don't come, as I've told them all about you."

"Oh, if we're only there for a few hours I'll be the life and soul of the party."

"We just say the soul of the party."

"Then I'll be that then," I said, giving her a grateful squeeze.

# 4

As I sat squeezed between Inma's auntie and cousin on her parent's sofa at 1.30pm on Saturday, I'd not yet had the chance to become the soul of the party, as during the hour we'd been there I'd scarcely spoken. After being introduced to her mother, father, two aunts, one uncle, three cousins and a small mongrel called Duke (pronounced 'Dook'), I'd done more smiling than talking, as the volume of chatter was far too high for me to get a word in edgeways. This did allow me to observe the progenitors of my beloved, however, who seemed like a steady, well-bred couple who took care of themselves, as they were both fairly trim and looked young for their ages of sixty-nine (father) and sixty-seven (mother). He'd worked in a bank and she in a haberdashery, and their flat was a spacious one in the Infante area to the south of the sluggish River Segura.

Murcia is a city of some 400,000 souls and as we drove in it seemed like a vast metropolis to a person who had only visited cities when it had been unavoidable, and the countless blocks of flats didn't appeal to me at all. Inma promised to show me the charming squares in the centre another day, but just then, beaming inanely from the sofa and faced with several hours of irksome social intercourse, I was looking forward to leaving the place.

"Where's Natalia?" I called to Inma as she passed by with two glasses of wine.

"Late."

At the time it felt like a minor consolation that her darling daughter would be unlikely to be able to give me the third degree among that buzzing throng, but in the event it was her who smoothed the way to a passably pleasant day for me. No sooner had she arrived at 1.55pm – having come by train from her father's flat in Alicante – than she pulled me up and dragged me into the adjoining dining room, where the table was already crammed with festive nibbles.

"Hola, Natalia," I said when she finally released my hand.

"I want a word with you, Alan," she said, her sharp brown eyes peering at me from beneath her new fringe.

"Yes, I gathered that. Oughtn't you to greet everyone first?"

"I know them all only too well, and there'll be time enough for pointless chatter later. I believe you've begun work on the hotel."

"Yes, well, the builders have. I was there yesterday and they're working like demons. They've already ripped up the tiles in the–"

"Good, so I expect it'll open on schedule."

"Yes, I think so. Why do you ask?"

"I'm interested in what you do, Alan." She smiled ingratiatingly. "I often ask after you when I speak to Mamá on the phone."

"Yes, and I always ask her what you've been up to. How are your studies going?"

She frowned. "I believe you'll have a key role in the hotel once it opens."

"Oh, I don't know about that. They want me to do something, but I don't know what yet," I said, wondering where this was going.

"You'll probably be in charge of the place."

"Oh, I doubt it, and I don't think I'd want to be anyway. I'm not a hotel manager."

"You can do anything if you put your mind to it, Alan."

"Perhaps, but I don't wish to run a hotel."

Her bottom lip jutted out and she blew on her fringe. "I'd like you to find me a job at the hotel, Alan."

"Ah, yes, well, they'll be busy in summer, hopefully, so I could ask Angela, the owner, if she needs anyone then."

"No, I mean a full-time job."

I gawped. "What? What do you mean?"

"I'm fed up of studying, Alan. I've grown out of it already and it's leading me nowhere."

"But I thought you wanted to become an anthropologist and travel the world."

She angrily swept back her fringe, which didn't suit her anyway. "Pah, that's just an empty dream."

"But why?"

"I met an anthropology graduate before Christmas, working in a *shop*. He saw a book I was carrying and told me that he'd finished his degree four years ago."

"And?"

"He told me it was hopeless, that there are never any jobs or research posts. He pointed out that the whole department are old people of over forty who are just clinging to their jobs."

"But that's just your university."

"He applied for posts all over Spain and didn't even get an interview."

I remembered Inma telling me that when she finished her psychology degree she knew there was little hope of finding relevant working. I also recalled her telling me that her daughter was far keener than she had been. Just then she entered the room, but on seeing Natalia's gloomy face and me scratching my head, she halted.

"We'll want to come in here soon," she said softly, leaving a bowl of salad on the end of the table.

"Ten minutes, Mamá."

"All right," she said, pulling the door to behind her.

During those few seconds my brain went into overdrive and I cleared my throat in preparation for my pep talk.

I smiled. "Well, Natalia, do you know what I think?" I said, buying myself a few more seconds.

"What?"

"Que tú y yo… that you and I must speak English together from now on," I said, switching to it in mid-sentence.

"What's *that* got to do with anything?" she said scornfully in Spanish.

"A lot," I said in English. "This former student you spoke to in the shop, does he speak good English?"

"I don't know," she said in English.

"Ha, I bet he doesn't. Your English is quite good, but you need to become fluent before you finish your studies. That way a whole *world* of opportunities will be open to you, literally."

She sniffed. "Hmm."

"I'm sure that out in the… field, English is the main language," I said, having seen archaeology and other documentaries in which folk from several non-English speaking countries chatted away in that tongue.

"Yes, I believe it is."

"Well then?"

"Oh, I'm just a little tired of it all. The lectures, my own projects, always anthropology all the time. I have no time for anything else," she said, still in English.

"I think you need to relax a little. You have over three years still to go. Leave your projects for now and just do the course. Meet some different people, go out more, do some exercise, disconnect," I said, warming to my subject, but fearing the usual rebuff.

She pursed her lips, then tutted pensively seven or eight times. "Well, perhaps I am being a little…"

"Hasty?"

"Yes, hasty. I think I do need to meet different people. The other students in the faculty are quite depressed."

"Depressed or depressing?"

"Depressing. They don't really expect to become anthropologists. They joke about what they will do when they finish. They think life is a game, or that their parents will look after them forever."

"Your English is really good, and I bet theirs isn't. Just take it easier for a while, then in the last year start applying for jobs and postgraduate courses everywhere." I heard shuffling outside and feared a stampede of hungry relatives. "The world is your oyster, Natalia."

"Yes, I know. Thank you, Alan, you've made me feel more positive."

"I…er, hope so," I said, her inscrutable expression making me still fear a dismissive quip.

"Let's sit down, as I want to speak more to you," she said, pulling back a chair about halfway down the long table, ushering me onto it, and sitting by my side. "Enter!" she cried in Spanish, whereupon they all loped or shuffled in.

Inma placed her cardigan on the back of the chair next to mine, before helping her mother and a sprightly aunt to bring in the platters of meat – both cooked and cured – and dishes of vegetables. A brief hush fell while everyone served themselves, but conversations were soon resumed, including mine with Natalia.

"In summer I had intended to do more anthropological research," she said as she filled my wine glass.

"Yes, perhaps we ought to speak Spanish now."

"But now I think I will have a complete break," she went on in English.

"Yes, good idea."

"And do something completely different."

"Yes, you should do that."

"Like work at the hotel."

I nodded, before knocking back half a glass of wine.

She squeezed my forearm. "I'm sure you'll be able to arrange that for me, Alan."

"I'll try."

"Because all life experience is anthropological, isn't it?"

"Er, yes."

"Good, that is settled. We can speak Spanish now," she said, and when I declared that she smoothed the way to a pleasantly passable day it was from this point that I meant, as sandwiched between her and her mother I was able to enjoy the delicious meal, followed by the typical *Roscón de Reyes*, a circular sweet-loaf containing little ceramic figures of the Three Kings, the Virgin Mary, sundry angels and, strangely enough, a kangaroo.

"Take care not to eat any figures you find, Alan," said Natalia prior to their gradual revelation. "Because grandmother uses them every year."

"OK."

"And watch out for the dried bean. It wasn't found last year and we think Uncle Prudencio ate it on purpose," she murmured.

I glanced over at the tubby, red-faced man. "Does he like dried beans?"

"No, but whoever finds it is supposed to pay for the roscón, and he's very mean."

In the event, Auntie Kika – short for Francisca – found the bean, which was all right, Natalia whispered, as she owned property and was reputed to be loaded.

Thus it was that my time at table passed agreeably, as when Natalia wasn't amusing me with mainly malicious gossip, Inma was gradually introducing me to her extended family, so when we finally rose to drink our glasses of cava wherever we wished, I felt relaxed and happy to have a chat with Inma's father, his sister María, the sprightly aunt, and her son Arturo, who was nothing like *my* Arturo, being a sombre, reserved sort of chap who worked as a truck mechanic. We'd remained in the dining room and conversation was general, until Arturo wandered away and Auntie María decided to go and help in the kitchen, when it suddenly became a lot more specific.

"So, Alan, you and Inma seem very happy together," said the lean, grey-haired man with the same sincere eyes as his daughter.

"Yes, we are, very happy."

"Good."

"Yes."

"She was unhappy."

"I know."

"But since meeting you, she's been happy."

"Yes."

"Her marriage was a difficult one."

"Yes, I believe so."

"You seem more relaxed and attentive than he ever was."

"I… yes." I sipped my cava. "Your daughter is a wonderful woman."

"Yes, she is. We've always been proud of her."

"Me too, since I met her, I mean," I said, beginning to feel distinctly hot under my soft collar, as Inma had told me that casual dress was fine, which was just as well, as I didn't possess a tie.

"I expect her divorce will come through soon."

"Yes, sometime this year, she hopes."

His bushy grey brows rose and fell in the blink of an eye. "I expect you're looking forward to that moment."

"I… yes, I am."

"Good, so tell me about these old coins that you sell."

Relieved, I rambled on about numismatic matters for a while, impressed by the fairly subtle way he'd hinted at his – and presumably his wife's – feelings regarding our unmarried state. Though neither of them were regular churchgoers, they'd obviously prefer us to cement our ties in the eyes of society, but until a date was set for the divorce – which her ex had acquiesced to calmly enough, Inma had told me – there was little point in talking about it. Me being me, however, and this coming hot on the heels of Zefe's helpful advice, I knew I'd fret about it until one or other of us brought up the subject. It was this damn house-ownership business that was still worrying me, you see, and the fact that I'd brought far less to our partnership than she had, so I'd just have to hope that things went well for me financially during the coming year.

"I've got a Spanish doubloon that might interest you, Alan," Inma's father said, as I'd been having the above thoughts, or some of them, while droning on about coins.

"Oh, yes?"

"Yes, just a moment."

Or maybe I should mention marriage sooner rather than later, just to gauge her reaction, I thought as I waited.

"Here it is."

I slipped the coin from its plastic pouch and held it up to the light. "Ah, yes, Carlos IV, 1791. Hispania and the Indies, it says, so probably made at the Potosi mint in Bolivia," I said, as although no expert in Spanish coins, I had done a little homework during the last few months.

"Potosi, that's right, or so my father told me."

"How did he come by the coin?"

"Oh, it's been in the family for a long time. How much do you think it's worth?"

"Oh, I'm not sure, but at least a couple of thousand, if not more. It's in very good condition."

"Yes, I had it valued at about three thousand only last year." He flicked it into the air, caught it, slipped it back into the pouch and smiled. "Enough to pay for a modest wedding, I think," he said, before winking and wandering out.

I was gazing out of the window at the darkening city when I felt a gun in my back.

'All right, we'll get married,' I was about to say, when I turned to find Natalia with two fingers still outstretched.

"I'm going now, Alan," she said in Spanish.

"Oh, back to Alicante?"

"No, straight to Madrid. I have work to do before the term starts."

"Course work?"

"Yes, I've been neglecting it while heating my head with a study of the African immigrants in the south-east of Madrid. I'll drop that for now and just go to lectures and write my essays."

"Yes, you do that. Don't you want to come to stay for a few days? I can drive you to Elda station whenever you want."

No, I'd better get back. Good luck with the hotel."

"Thanks."

"I'll be able to start work in about the middle of June."

I gulped, as I often do in Natalia's presence. "I'll mention you to Angela when I see her."

She kissed me hard on just the one cheek. "I know you will. See you in a few weeks."

"Bye, Natalia."

"Did you have an awful time dear?" Inma said as we trundled along the dual-carriageway in my Clio, her hatchback being a little the worse for wear by then.

"Not at all," I said, before summarising my chat with Natalia and omitting to mention her father's hints.

"Yes, I just told her not to be so silly, but I think you were more constructive, as she told me in no uncertain terms." She giggled. "She's beginning to respect you now, I think."

"Hmm, er, Inma?"

"Yes?"

"Do you think we ought to get married sometime, in the future, I mean."

She shrugged and patted my leg. "We could do, if you like. I don't really mind."

I breathed a huge, audible sigh of relief. "Good, then we can talk about it at a later date."

She laughed. "Ha, has Papá been getting at you?"

"Oh, not really, just a hint."

"Well Mamá's been quite annoying about it, and I'm not even divorced yet."

"What did you say to her?"

"I told her that we were already married in each other's eyes, and that was what mattered."

I smiled. "Yes, I like that, in each other's eyes." I listened to the purr of the engine for a while. "In that case, I'd like to make you a wedding gift."

"What for? The lovely bracelet you gave me can be a wedding gift, if you like."

"We're going to buy you a new car."

"Oh, mine's all right."

"No, it's too old for all the kilometres you do now. We'll get Bernie to find us a newish one and pay for it from the cornflakes box."

"All right then, but nothing fancy."

"I like the watch you gave me," I said, jingling it, as we'd exchanged gifts towards the end of the get-together.

She chuckled. "It'll go well with your document case, now that you're an executive."

"Ha, yes. I wonder when I'll see my bosses, and where they'll stay."

"Don't worry about that now."

"No, I won't."

# 5

"Oh, can I not stay here, Alan? The weather's so lovely just now," said Zefe on Tuesday morning when I went to turf him out of the annex.

"What, while I'm slaving away in your damn flat?" I said, before recalling Juan's lukewarm response to his ripping yarns when they'd first met. I'd seen Juan in the bar the previous day, you see, and not only had he agreed to oversee the patio, steps and railings job, but had also offered to take a peek at my proposed work at Zefe's.

"Aw, alright, I'll pack my things then," he said, shading his eyes from the sun I was about to deprive him of, as his first floor flat got no sunlight whatsoever in winter.

As he hobbled inside like a hundred-year-old, I relented. "All right, give me your keys, but I'm driving you down on Thursday."

The old devil turned and beamed at me. "Oh, Alan, you're making my waning years so much more bearable than they would have been. If I were a religious man I'd say that you were well on the way to sainthood."

"Yes, Saint Muggins of Lancashire," I muttered in English, before surveying the living and kitchenette area. "You could give this place a dust and a sweep, you know."

"Yes, yes, I will, later. There are the keys," he said, before prising off his slippers with his stick.

"In a hurry?"

"What? No, no."

"Going to enjoy the sunshine in Álvaro's den, are you?"

"I may call round later, yes," he said, dragging a shoe towards him.

"Why don't you invite him up here and sit in the sun for a while," I said, as after a cold night it really was going to be a wonderfully still and sunny day.

"There's only one comfortable chair for sitting outside, Alan."

"I'll get you another one."

"Thank you, Alan."

"Shall I bring our sofa too?"

"No, Alan, another chair will be fine."

"Good."

On fetching the folding chair he asked if I'd mind calling on Álvaro and informing him of their change of venue. "He'll know which books to bring," he added.

I scraped my foot on the stony ground like an impatient stallion. "No, you can walk there. You need the exercise."

"All right, Alan. Will we be going swimming on Thursday then?"

I grasped my head. "Yes, no… I don't know," I muttered.

"Or on Friday, if you prefer."

"Adiós, Zefe," I said as I turned and jogged away.

"Be careful when you move the bookcase, Alan, as those books are precious to me," he yelled as I hurtled through the gate.


"Where's the old goat, then?" Juan asked me when I'd shown him the tiles which I proposed to stick to the floor with geometrical precision.

"Sunbathing on his country estate."

"Good, he's an old bore."

Although I'd expected Juan to sit in one of the easy chairs we'd once brought in his van and give me instructions, he'd arrived at the bar dressed in faded blue overalls, toting an iron bar with which he playfully tickled Jesús between the legs.

"Hey, don't touch me there of all places, you big oaf."

"No, not there," said Vicente. "Or you'll start him off again and I'll have to throw him out."

"Vicente won't allow me to talk about my... condition here anymore," Jesús told us.

"Thank God," said Juan.

"As he thinks he'll lose customers, but I tell him that he'll lose more customers to... you know, if they don't follow my advice and examine themselves thoroughly every morning."

"Je-sús," Vicente growled.

He raised his hands. "That's all I have to say."

"Why are you still here at this time?" I asked him, as it was almost ten o'clock.

"Still here? I've already been on my land for hours. The truth is that there's little to do right now, so I've come to cheer everybody up."

Vicente groaned.

"Why don't you come to help me and Juan do a bit of work on a poor old man's flat?" I asked.

"I'll let you wield my tool if you come," Juan said, waving it about.

"No thanks, there's always ploughing to do."

I waited for him to enquire about Bernie's tractor or field, but the selfish old sod didn't, so we finished our coffee and headed off.

I'd brought half my armoury of building equipment along, but Juan just had the extremely long chisel, and while I was carting my stuff up the stairs he'd grabbed a hammer and was making short work of the skirting tiles. We then emptied the room of furniture and set about the floor tiles, most of which came off with a couple of light blows.

"I thought they'd be harder to get off," I said as we toiled.

"No, for many years now the Spanish builder has worked fast, especially on flats."

"I hope they do a good job at the hotel. They'll also be laying some tiles today, I think," I said, having asked Arturo to apprise me of any issues.

"Cristóbal will do a good enough job, I'm sure. What will you do there when it opens, Alan?"

"I don't know. I don't really want to work there full-time," I said, having given some thought to the matter since Natalia had suggested I might end up managing the place. "I'd like to do something interesting that won't tie me down all the time."

He straightened up and wiped his sweaty brow. "You like your freedom, don't you, Alan?"

"Yes."

"Quite right. Sell your coins and look out for more house buyers. You have no need to become an employee now."

"No. What have you been up to?"

"Oh, getting a little bored, to be honest, but I hope to do some more driving soon."

"For the furniture company?"

"Perhaps, but an old friend was home in the holidays. He has lived in Vitoria for many years."

"Ah, in the Basque Country?"

"Yes. He has a company which manufactures components for the automotive industry. He asked me if I was still driving and I told him I was, for friends. He may wish me to do a few trips, from Vitoria to Valencia, Alicante and Murcia."

"Does he not have his own vans?"

"Of course, and he uses transport companies, but the truth is that I expressed a certain willingness to deliver his goods and as I'm an old friend he was happy to give me some work." He shrugged. "He doesn't *need* me, but he's more than happy for me to do a few trips. He's only three years younger than me and still works hard, so he understands why I get bored." He shrugged again. "Ha, if I were a more imaginative man like you, Alan, I might have more to do."

"You could do some spor... exercise. Walking, or even cycling. You told me you used to cycle a lot."

He cradled his considerable paunch and shook his head. "I don't think so, Alan. It would be unseemly for a man of my age to go cycling."

"Not in my country."

"Anyway, I've come here to do some exercise," he said, before laying into the remaining tiles with a vengeance.

When we'd finished he asked me where my *capazos* were. Capazos are the large, rubbery tubs with handles and I'd brought a single one in which to pour the mortar. I pointed at it.

"That little thing? We need big ones to carry this rubble down to the van, and then to mix the material in."

"Ah, but I've bought this special mortar for the tiles," I said, pointing to a tub.

He shook his head. "Then this will be the most expensive floor since they laid the tiles in the great mosque of Córdoba. What did you and Arturo use when tiling your little house?"

"Er, sand, cement, and something else, but the lad at the builders' merchant's recommended this stuff."

"That stuff is for small surfaces, and for guiris." He sighed and took out his phone.

When I'd carted most of the old tiles down to Juan's van, another van arrived with bags of sand and cement and two huge capazos. Juan emerged with a tub of mortar.

"Take this back and he'll come to reckon up later," he said to the driver.

"OK," he said, and was off.

"We'll use the other tub for coating the back of the tiles."

"All right."

I can see that I'm in danger of giving you a blow by blow account of the tiling of a floor, so I'll skip the mundane stuff and move on to the point where I brought up the subject of Juan's Vitoria trips again. By that time we'd chipped away some of the old cement and had begun to spread the new stuff (me), and lay tiles (Juan).

"Won't they be rather long trips for you, Juan?"

"Yes, but better long trips than none at all. Vitoria is about seven hundred kilometres from here, so I'll drive up one day and back down the next, via Valencia. Then on the third day I'll make the deliveries to Alicante and Murcia."

"Can't you make all the deliveries on the second day?"

He smiled and shook his head. "Not alone, no. It would be too much for me."

"I'll come with you then."

"Oh, no, Alan, you're far too busy now."

"It's only two days, and I am my own boss, remember? You don't have to pay me, as I'm keen to see the north anyway."

He chuckled. "My friend will pay me well, I'm sure, and I'm not really doing it for the money either, so there'll be enough for both of us."

"Where will we stay overnight?"

"At my friend's house, of course. His wife is Basque and a very good cook."

"Great. Tell me as soon as you know the dates."

"All right. Pass me two more tiles and some spacers."

Thursday was a busy day for me, as after prising Zefe out of the annex I drove him home, mopped the new floor, carted his furniture back into place, took him swimming, allowed him to invite me to lunch at a decent restaurant, took him home again, and finally made it out to the hotel at about five o'clock.

"Been having a nice time while we've been working like blacks?" Cristóbal mumbled with a screw in his mouth, as he was removing a door.

"Yes," I said, resisting a strong impulse to show him my slightly blistered hands. "Is everything going well?"

He glared at me, twisting the screw between his lips like Clint Eastwood's cheroot in those spaghetti westerns. "You don't need to ask."

"I have to ask."

"See for yourself."

"I have. I'm amazed by how much work has been done."

He grunted amiably. "I think your bosses will be pleased when they come next week."

"Next week?"

"Do you never read your emails, Alan?"

"Not since this morning."

"Did you buy your phone in the Stone Age?"

My mobile was still the same basic one that I'd 'borrowed' from Cathy and Bernie not long after we'd arrived at their house. "About then, yes."

"Ha, some executive you are," he said, spitting out the screw.

I looked at my executive watch and stroked my executive document case. Inma had used the word not long before and the more I heard it, the less I wanted to be one. If I really became an executive, how could I shoot off with Juan on trips to the north or do other interesting things on a whim?

"What did he say in the email?"

"*She* said that they'd be arriving next Wednesday afternoon, and more stuff that I couldn't be bothered to read. Look, it's addressed to you anyway." He handed me his dusty smartphone.

Angela, in an email about twenty times the length of Malcolm's usual notes, said that she was very excited about visiting her project, but that Malcolm still hadn't told her where they'd be staying. She hoped that I'd be there on Wednesday, as she wished to discuss her ideas for the hotel with me, now that the opening date was drawing nearer, etc, etc.

"Hmm," I handed back the phone. "Six days from now. Could you, er… finish a suite or something, so they can see what they'll look like?"

"No, I have a plan, and I'm sticking to it."

"I thought you might say that. They're going to be impressed anyway, so we needn't worry."

"Do I look worried?" he said with a fierce and unworried grimace.

"Keep up the good work," I said, patting him paternally on the shoulder, before marching purposefully from the room.

I found Arturo and Diego just outside the main door, mixing cement for the skilled workers.

"Everything OK?" I asked.

Diego straightened up and puffed out his cheeks. "Cristóbal's become more of a slave driver than ever. He's got us working eleven hours like the bloody Manchegos."

"And this weekend too, as they're not going home," said Arturo almost gleefully. He patted his brother-in-toil on the back. "Cheer up and think about the money."

"My bloody wife keeps it all. She doesn't trust me with it."

Arturo grasped his arm. "You mustn't drink, Diego, or not much. Follow my example and you'll be all right."

"Hmm."

Had Arturo mauled Diego like that a few weeks earlier he'd probably have called him a gypsy swine, but he now seemed content enough to work alongside the effusive chap, though he tried not to show it. Vicente had told me that Diego rarely got drunk anymore, at least not in his bar, and that his previously stormy family life appeared to have settled down. Arturo seemed to be positively thriving on all the hard work, and I asked him if he didn't miss the markets that he'd begun to visit again after being forced to stay away for a while due to selling a dodgy car to some 'bad' gypsies.

"Not at all, Alan. Here I come, work and make money, whereas there I go, set up at some ungodly hour, and then stand around all day hoping to sell my stuff."

"But on the markets you can use your eloquence and talk to lots of people all day long."

"Yes, but always trying to sell. Here I can use my eloquence on my colleagues, eh, Diego?"

Diego grunted.

"On the markets I'm a gypsy and here I'm a payo, or try to be. On the whole I prefer to be a payo at work and a gypsy at play. A good life balance, eh?"

"Yes, I guess so. How's your daughter?"

"Rocío is fine, thanks, but will miss her Dad this weekend, as I'll be here."

"That's a shame."

He shrugged. "No matter. I can now buy her everything she needs," he said, before beginning to fill a fresh cement mixer. The afternoon was turning chilly, but he was still dressed in a vest and his dark arms seemed more sinewy than ever, the veins standing out on his fine biceps. When Diego wheeled a barrowful of material to the men inside I asked him if everyone seemed happy on the job.

He poured a final bucketful of water in and switched on the mixer, before fishing his cigarettes from his back pocket and lighting one. We stepped away from the building and I saw lights on in half a dozen rooms, or ex-rooms, as parts of the place were still awaiting new walls and everything else.

"Yes, I think so. The Manchegos are used to this kind of work. They're tough men and they rarely complain. They have everything they need for the evenings now, including televisions, so it's just business as usual for them."

"And Cristóbal's boys?"

"Oh, they tend to moan a little, especially about the long hours, but this weekend they'll all be here, as they too like to earn money after some lean times."

"The following weekend they can rest when the Manchegos go home," I said, feeling like a lazybones in the company of so many grafters.

"Yes. Hey, do you think the owners will want to have a small house here? Cristóbal seems to think we'll be staying here to build it."

"I don't know, Arturo. Next Wednesday we might find out."

# 6

The following Wednesday I was on site by twelve and rushed inside through the pouring rain, using my document case as an umbrella. Both teams' cement mixers were rumbling away in what was to become the foyer and I found Cristóbal upstairs, giving instructions to Rafael, the head Manchego.

"Hola, Alan," said he.

"Hola, how's this cabrón treating you all?" I said, as I tried to utter a few manly vulgarities on each visit.

"We've had worse bosses, and we're off home for a rest at lunchtime on Friday."

"Are you excited about seeing Malcolm and Angela?" I asked Cristóbal.

"Do I look excited?" he growled. "Have you mentioned the new house we're building them yet?"

I twisted my neck to hide the inevitable gulp. "Not exactly."

"Not ex*act*ly?"

"Well, as there's this big mystery about where they'll be staying, it didn't seem appropriate to mention it," I said, grasping my document case and trying not to cringe.

"Pah, some mystery! They'll be staying at a hotel, of course," he said before stomping off.

"A pleasant man," I said to Rafael.

"Oh, he's all right. He's just a little timid, that's all."

"Timid?"

"Yes, that's at the root of his grumpiness. He may be a younger child whose older siblings made him feel inferior." He shrugged and twiddled his trowel. "Who knows? I just know that he pays us every week and is managing the project well. The other day he took Anacleto to the dentist's."

Anacleto was the oldest of the Manchegos, apart from Rafael himself, and I remarked that it had been unusually considerate of Cristóbal.

"Yes, well, he wanted him to get his tooth extracted so that he could go on working, but he wouldn't let him pay the bill."

"Ah, he's got a heart of gold. Oh, it sounds like a van's arriving," I said, wandering over to the window. "Bloody hell," I said in English.

Rafael joined me. "I think it's some kind of bus."

I gazed down at the rain-streaked silver roof and put two and two together.

"Es una autocaravana," I said, meaning motorhome.

"It's a big one," said Rafael.

"Malcolm's a big man."

"The owner of this place?"

"Yes, him and his wife."

The van circled and came to rest on the gravel right next to the tiled area leading to the pool. Rooted to the spot, I was expecting the driver's door to open, but instead my phone rang.

"Hello."

"Alan, are you here?" my master's voice roared.

"Yes, I…"

"Come outside. I have a surprise for you."

"I can see it."

"Well come here. I want to talk to you." He hung up.

I trotted down the stairs and into the rain. On approaching the van, the side door swung open.

"Come in, come in, Alan," the big man boomed, smiling from ear to ear. "Wipe your feet," he said as he grasped my hand and pulled me in.

"Well, this is a surprise. Hello, Angela."

"Hi, Alan. A cup of tea?"

"Yes, please. Don't you want to see the work first?"

"That can wait," Malcolm said, propelling me to a cosy nook with a small round table. "Sit down. What do you think of her then?"

Assuming he meant the van, I said it was even more impressive inside than out.

"Yes, only the best is good enough for my Angela."

She brought the mugs of tea and sat down with us. "I knew nothing until this morning, Alan. When the taxi took us to a huge place near Elche with dozens of motorhomes I thought we were just going to look, but they drove this one round and before I knew it we were off to a hypermarket to buy everything we needed."

Malcolm's huge head was nodding. "I planned it all meticulously, Alan. After I'd decided that I didn't want us to live in there, I got thinking and came up with this simple solution. When we come over we can stay here, and if we get bored we can shoot off wherever we want."

"Oh, so are you not driving it… her back to England?"

"No, she'll stay here. You'll keep an eye on her, won't you?"

"Of course. What make is she?"

"She's a Hymer B-class Supreme… something or other. The best they had in stock, and she didn't come cheap, but we'll get some use out of her, won't we, love?"

"We certainly will. She drives really well for such a big van, Alan, and I'm sure we'll visit lots of places."

"Yes, it'll be great," I said, glad that she really seemed to like it after not having been consulted in the matter.

"Years and years ago we had a little Volkswagen camper van and we went all over Britain in it, until Malcolm became too busy to take proper holidays."

"Ah, I see. We could get Cristóbal to put outdoor plug sockets near to wherever you're going to park her."

"Good idea, Alan," he said, before his mighty brow creased. "I'm glad you're keeping us up to date on the work, because that Christabel doesn't seem to be able to write more than a sentence."

"Yes, Cristóbal's a man of few words, but plenty of action. The whole team are working like mad and I'm sure it'll be finished before the end of April."

"I expected nothing less," he said, before draining his mug. "Come on, let's have a look then."

We scurried into the house and I expected Cristóbal to be there to receive us, but as he wasn't I led them around the ground floor, making pertinent comments. Angela said hola to the workers we came across, many of whom gawped at the giant who just nodded or grunted, clearly taking everything in. When they saw Rafael and David's bedroom, the other one being upstairs at the time, neither of them seemed to mind. We found Cristóbal waiting at the top of the main stairs, his dark hair speckled with dust. He wiped his right hand on his overalls and grasped Malcolm's great paw, before smiling and nodding at Angela.

"So you muck in too, do you, Chris?" Malcolm said.

"What?"

"You also work, with your hands," I clarified.

"Of course." He looked at Malcolm. "The work goes good. Little to see now, but going good."

"I can see that."

"Have you made progress with the paperwork?" Angela said.

"I had, but with this change in plans, now I start again, but no problem," he said, daring to give Malcolm a slightly irritated look.

The big man clapped him on the shoulder. "You're making enough money out of this, so get it done, lad."

"Yes, no problem. Come, I show you the work here," he said, before guiding us around the first floor, making brief, grammar-free comments until we reached the easternmost part of the house, where he pointed out of the window. "That is best place to build little chalet for you, about thirty metres from hotel."

"Haven't you seen our van, man?" said M.

"Yes, nice autocaravana. Good for now, and big, but small to live. A house better, in future."

"Yes, well, shall we go down?" I said, not wishing him to test Malcolm's patience.

"First the hotel, Chris, then we'll see, eh?" he said, amused rather than annoyed.

"What would you like to do now?" I asked them as we descended the stairs.

"We'll go somewhere for lunch," said Malcolm.

I nodded and began to fish out my car keys.

"Not in that little thing. Here, drive us somewhere nice."

I came to a halt with the shiny Hymer keys in my hand. "Er, I wouldn't want to scratch it."

"Don't be soft. I want to see how it feels to be a passenger."

I glanced at Angela.

She smiled. "You drive there and I'll drive back. He won't be happy until we've both told him how wonderfully she handles. Don't worry, she's fully insured."

"She handles wonderfully," I said as we approached the town, as it felt very much like driving Juan's van, though I kept reminding myself that it was much longer. I chose a smart restaurant on the outskirts with a big car park and it was with some relief that I handed back the keys and led them inside.

Over lunch we talked about the work on the hotel and Angela described how she'd like the grounds to look.

"I want to have lawns on either side of the pool, and I'd like to clear the ground under those pine trees, plant some more, and put a few benches there. I want my guests to be able to go off alone to read, draw or just think."

"She's still convinced that she'll get lots of arty types to come, Alan," Malcolm said with a grin.

I knew better than to grin back. "Hmm, is that artist you mentioned still going to come, Angela?"

"Not that one, but another is provisionally booked from the fifth to the thirteenth of May."

I nodded. "Oh, that's very soon after opening, isn't it?"

"I plan to open on the sixth. The staff will start before then, to train and get everything ready, then if all goes to plan we'll open with a full house. I want the staff to see that I mean business, so they'll tell everyone how quickly we filled up. As soon as Tina signs her contract I'll start advertising the course. I'll call it something simple like 'Painting and drawing retreat in southern Spain,' and make the first one quite affordable. Tina's done courses of this type before, so I can leave it to her to organise it."

"What kind of artist is she?"

"A fairly conventional one. She paints portraits on commission and things like that." She tittered. "Malcolm didn't like the sound of the first one I considered, did you, dear?"

"Hmm, her paintings looked like the work of a raving lunatic and her sculptures were just piles of stones."

"She's well thought of."

"Not by me. This Tina seems more like my cup of tea."

"Where will you advertise?" I asked.

"In *The Guardian*, I think," she said.

"Flaming lefties' rag," said Malcolm mildly.

"And *The Telegraph*. I'd like to get a good mix and give them a wonderful experience, so that they'll talk about it too."

All this seemed rather ambitious to me, but she appeared to be sure of herself, and as financial backing wouldn't be lacking my thoughts turned to what role she might have in mind for me. As I've said, I had no wish to commit myself to the venture on a full-time basis and suffer the drudgery I'd so far avoided in my singularly undynamic life. I'd have preferred to speak about it alone with her, lest Malcolm lumber me with undesirable tasks, but as procrastination would only make me fret about my destiny, over coffee I broached the subject in my inimitably forthright way.

"So, er... Angela, what, er... do you have in mind for me once the hotel opens, if anything?"

She chuckled. "What do you have in mind for yourself, Alan?"

"Well, er... maybe to keep an eye on things, like I'm doing now."

"Do you want to manage the place?" Malcolm said brusquely.

"No. No, I–"

"Thought not. We'll need someone experienced anyway, as we're not planning to stick around all the time."

"Unless there's a course on, dear."

"Unless there's a course on."

"Why don't we just wait and see, Alan?" Angela said. "It would be good if you didn't make any other plans for late April and May, then we could take it from there."

"Yes, that might be best."

Malcolm finished his coffee and sighed contentedly. "I'm satisfied that Chris is doing a good job, but do pop round at least once a week, there's a good lad."

"Yes, and I could start the van if you like."

"Yes." He narrowed his eyes and gazed at me with his chin in his hand, rocking his head from side to side. "You ought to take a holiday, you know. Get away somewhere with that lovely girl of yours."

"Yes, we might."

"Before we open."

"Before we open, yes. I'll be heading up north soon, with my friend Juan, in his van, to pick up some goods," I said, to show him that I was a man of action.

"Good for you. We're going to head south now, to try to find some warmer weather."

"Are you not sticking around for a while?"

"What for? I'll have another look around this aft, then tomorrow we'll be off at the crack of dawn, for a week or so, then we'll come back and leave the van."

"I'll drive you to the airport."

"Thanks." He picked up the keys and swung them to and fro before my eyes, grinning like a well-fed hippopotamus.

"Yes, I'll start her up regularly after you've gone home."

"Take a trip in her sometime, Alan."

I smiled like a petrified dolphin. "Oh, no, I wouldn't... I couldn't..."

He raised a finger as big as a small child's arm. "I didn't pay over a hundred grand for a van just to have her sat there most of the time."

"I... well..."

"Don't lend her to anyone else though."

"I..."

"You could go away with your sister and brother-in-law," said Angela. "It easily sleeps four."

"Well, that's very kind of you both," I said, blushing like a virgin bride.

"It's because we trust you, Alan," he said.

"I appreciate it."

"To look after the van."

"Yes."

"And to make sure the hotel's finished in good time."

"Yes."

"Oh, see about those lawns that Angela mentioned, will you?"

"Yes, though it's a bit cold now."

"April will do. Get them to bring them in rolls, you know, and send me the bill."

"We'll do a sketch when we get back, Alan, now that it's finally stopped raining."

"Yes," I said.

"But don't turn into one of those bloody yes-men, Alan," said he.

"No."

"Drive us back. Angela can have a go tomorrow."

"Ye... OK. I'll just pay the bill."

"I'll pay."

"No, *I'll* pay," I insisted.

"All right."

"How did it go?" Inma said when I walked through the door just after dark.

"Muy bien. Look at this," I said, showing her a blurred photo on my phone, a naff camera being one of its few advanced features.

"A big motorhome, outside the hotel. Is it theirs?"

"Yes," I said, before describing the events of the day over a cup of tea.

"I'm glad they're pleased with everything and that you haven't committed yourself to anything you'll regret," she said after hearing me out like a dutiful wife, I mean partner.

"Oh, no, I told them straight that I wasn't going to be a wage slave."

"A what?"

"Er, a person who goes to work for somebody else every day, I suppose."

"Like most people?"

"Yes, but, I mean, you don't want me to tie myself down at the hotel, do you?"

"Not really, or I'd scarcely see you in summer. Like Angela said, you'll just have to see how things develop."

"Yes, though from April I'd better be available. I thought we might take a holiday before then, maybe with Cathy and Bernie," I said, leading up to my momentous news.

She looked puzzled. "We could, I suppose."

I held up my phone and slowly brought it before her eyes, which I suppose was my idea of a kind of drum roll.

"We could go in *this*."

"What?"

I turned it round and saw that the screen was blank. After a prod I tried again.

"In this."

"In that?"

"Yes. Malcolm… they said we could use it."

She shrugged. "Hmm, that's nice of them."

"You don't sound too excited, Inma."

"I'm just concerned that you'll be so scared of bumping it that you won't be able to relax."

"Bernie can drive. He's never bumped a vehicle in his life, or so he says. If you want us to go with them, that is."

She smiled and grasped my hand. "I'd love to, in that or in the car."

"Oh."

"Alan, when I worked at the pharmaceutical company my boss once lent us a little motorboat that he kept in the marina at Denia, to use while we were on holiday, you know."

"Right... er, right."

"Natalia was small then and we had a great time speeding about in it."

"I see," I said, Inma's past life flashing before my eyes, but failing to see what she was leading up to.

"Yes, it was great, then when we got back to work in September I was asked to do all sorts of extra tasks and my husband's workload increased too. One has to be careful where bosses are concerned, Alan. They rarely give you something for nothing."

"Oh, I don't believe they think like that, not Angela anyway. Besides, they're not my bosses in the same way that yours was."

"True. Oh, Rosa says that Agustín wants to sell his Seat Ibiza. It's only three years old, but he's yearning for one of those Nissan Qashqais that seem to be fashionable now. I thought we might buy it. They just want the same amount as the dealer would give them."

I grasped her hand and smiled. "The cornflakes box is your oyster, my dear."

"Does the mean that we'll buy it?"

"Sí, cariño. Bernie can sell your old one. It'll give him something to do."

# 7

"What do you mean, it'll give me something to do? I'm rushed off my feet," Bernie said when I called him a few days later while gazing at our sleek blue Seat Ibiza – a 1.2 TSI with only 34,450km on the clock – over the patio wall. "And why haven't I seen the new car?"

"You were out yesterday when we called round in it at about five."

"I was on my field and Cathy had gone to yoga."

I realised that it had been a while since I'd called, despite my New Year's resolution to cycle over to lend a hand on the allotment every week. "Right, so you've got the field?"

"Yep."

"And Cathy's taken up yoga?"

"Correct. She's been three or four times and she loves it. I often find her tied up on her mat, practising."

"She was a flexible girl, as she did gymnastics, but is she still bendy enough to do yoga?"

"Why don't you come and ask her yourself?"

I heard Inma getting ready to leave. "Yes, I'll come over and spend the day with you."

"About time. If I'm not here I'll be at the field or in the bar."

While Inma drove her new car, I messed about with the baffling console.

She chuckled. "We'd better read the manual. I've never had such a modern car before."

"Bernie will find a buyer for the old one, as he can't really be all that busy."

"All right."

The bar was buzzing with breakfasting workers when we arrived at about half past ten, and while I was drinking coffee at the bar and catching up with old Juan Antonio, Randi arrived. Despite spending so much time with food, she'd lost a bit of weight and looked tanned, radiant and, I must say, extremely attractive, even in a duffle coat and woolly hat.

"How are you both?" I asked.

"We're well, but it's been cold, hasn't it? I've walked here very fast to warm myself up."

"It's been cold at night, yes, but I thought you'd be used to it, being from the frozen north."

"In Norway we had central heating," she said glumly.

"What are you using now then?"

"Gas heaters and a wood fire."

"A stove?"

"No, just a fire in the fireplace. Oh, Alan, the heat goes whoosh, straight up the chimney."

I tutted sympathetically. "No, you need to get a wood-burning stove, Randi. Much more efficient."

"I know. Bernie told me they've been using the stove all day long, as well as the air conditioning at times. I told Arvid and he just said that one has to be tough in the country, the foolish man. I'd better start work," she said, and entered the kitchen.

"What was all that?" said Juan Antonio.

"Sorry, we should have spoken Spanish. Oh, she says she's a bit cold in the house," I said, still rather stunned by her calling

Arvid foolish, as although he undoubtedly was, a few months earlier she wouldn't have dreamed of openly disparaging him.

The old man grinned mischievously. "In the house she may be cold, but she spends little enough time there."

"Always here, is she?"

"Here and elsewhere, but my lips are sealed," he murmured, his eyes implying that he wouldn't need much persuading to unseal them.

Just then Bernie arrived, but instead of making a beeline for his favourite brother-in-law he stopped to chat to two oldish men dressed in blue overalls like him, except that his were newer. Although they were speaking quietly I heard the words tractor, plough (noun), frost, rocks, plough (verb), olive trees, crazy foreigner, almond trees, and 'you'll see'.

"Juan Antonio, do the farmers here tease Bernie?"

"Tease him? I don't think so, no, as they always seem interested in what he has to say."

"Hmm," I said, tuning in again when he'd ambled out.

"…unpredictable… possibly… glut of almonds… international markets… probably… low prices… olives… olive oil… you'll see," were among the words that Bernie uttered as they huddled around him, scratching their heads or bellies. He then raised his hands, nodded his head, clapped them both on the back and wandered over.

"Putting them straight, were you?" I said.

"They resist change, poor men, but they're coming around to my way of thinking. Rosa, un cortado, por favor."

She smiled and nodded at the grizzled man of the soil, him having neglected to shave for a couple of days. "How's the car?" she asked me.

"Great. It's like new."

She sighed. "I know, but men are so foolish about cars. Agustín simply had to have that Japanese one."

"Better he buy some land and tractor," said Bernie, confirming my suspicion that although he seemed to speak Spanish with greater fluency, grammar was still an unopened book to him.

"He hasn't got time for that," she said.

Because he's working to pay for a twenty-odd grand car that he doesn't need, I thought but didn't say, as someone has to buy the new ones.

"The land is the future," Bernie told her. "When no electric or petrol, all go back to land."

"Yes, Bernie, you've already told me that," she said.

"I like to play the environmental catastrophist from time to time," he said outside the bar.

"What's the great Norwegian environmentalist up to now?" I said, still pondering on Juan Antonio's unsubtle hints regarding Randi's movements.

"Well, I suppose all his cycling makes him green, though his allotment's looking pretty green too, but not with vegetables."

"Weeds?"

"Yes. As far as I know he just works on his computer and spends the rest of the time cycling. The last time I saw him he said he'd soon be going to Tenerife to do some altitude training, the daft sod."

"Each to his own."

"Yes, but I mean, if he was young enough to become a pro cyclist I could understand it, but he's forty-odd. Seems like he's obsessive about it to me."

"He's that kind of person."

"Hmm, but while he's away, we'll see what his wife gets up to."

I just raised my brows, me not being a great gossip.

"Has Inma not said anything about her?" he asked.

"Only that she's a great cook."

"Well, do you remember that supposed ex-military man she'd been getting friendly with?"

"You mentioned him once."

"Well… oh, I can't be bothered talking about that. Ask Inma sometime. Let's go to my field."

"Where's your tractor?"

"Spartacus is there, eager for action. He's not road legal, remember, so I don't bring him here much, as the Guardia Civil sometimes drop in for coffee and I can't be sure they'll turn a blind eye."

"That's a shame, because it was your dream to drive down on the tractor to hang out with the other farmers, wasn't it?" I said, pointing to a big green tractor with number plates.

"Oh, I soon got over that, and the field's not really going to take up much of my time, not for a while, anyway. I still nip over to help Jesús now and then, but he doesn't really need me anymore. Nice grub though."

"You'll have time to sell that then," I said, pointing to Inma's dusty old car.

"Yes, leave it there. I'll soon get shut of it."

"What do you think of this little beauty?" I said as I opened the Ibiza's passenger door and ushered him in.

"It's all right. You know that new cars do nothing for me."

"Well Inma and I are very pleased with it."

"How many kilometres?"

I told him.

"Like new then. How much?"

I told him.

"A good buy, despite not consulting me. Come on."

We drove the two hundred yards to his field, which was roughly equidistant between the bar and the house.

"Wow, Spartacus is looking really good," I said, stroking the gleaming red paintwork.

"Yes, and wait till you hear him." He started it up. "What do you think?" he bellowed over the din.

"Er, I can't really hear the difference," I bellowed back.

"No tapping anymore, and look at the exhaust."

I observed the light-grey smoke belching out. "Yes, much better."

He turned the key, thank goodness. "Yes, his engine's had a complete overhaul and he sounds as good as new."

"Are many of your farmer friends hard of hearing?"

"Some, yes. Why do you ask?"

"Oh, no reason." I turned to the field, still a stony mass of weeds stretching away between two ploughed fields of almond trees. I clicked my tongue a few times.

"I know. My mate with the big tractor's a bit busy now, but he'll soon get round to it."

"Right. Oh, haven't you got your own plough yet?"

"Nearly. I've offered four hundred for one and I'm not budging."

"No, you wouldn't."

"Come on, Cathy's looking forward to seeing you."

"Hello, stranger," she said, not for the first time.

"Nice tights."

"I've been doing my yoga," she said, pointing to a mat between the sofa and the stove, which was glowing softly, most the vents being shut.

"Is the firewood lasting?" I asked them.

"Is it heck," said Bern. "We've just ordered another ton. It gets bloody cold here, especially when it's windy. How is it at the cave?"

I tried not to smile too smugly. "Oh, it's not too bad. We use the stove, but it soon gets too hot." I shrugged. "That's caves for you."

"Cool in summer and warm in winter," Cathy said before I had chance to. "I've been reading one of the books you gave me."

"Oh, which one?"

"Jekyll and Hyde."

"How is it?"

"Not too difficult if I keep glancing at the English text. I'll read the one with short stories next."

"I'll buy you a couple more, unless you feel ready to tackle a normal Spanish novel."

"No way. Far too hard."

"What about you, Bern?"

"What about me?"

"Don't you fancy having a go at a Spanish book?"

"Us farmers aren't that literate. We're tied to the land, you see."

"Yes. Oh, shall we do a bit on the allotment?"

"It's weed free. It's winter, remember. What are you going to do with your land?"

I pictured the petrified almond trees which punctuated the two strips of land that were every bit as rocky and weed-infested as Bernie's new field. I sighed.

"Oh, I don't know. Maybe I'll have a bright idea one day, but for now I'll just leave it. I think I'm going to be a busy man," I said, before telling them about the patio project which Juan was going to assist me with, plus the trips we hoped to make up north.

"Ah, the north. We're driving up there when the weather gets better," said Bernie. "Seeing as we missed out last summer and went to bloody England instead."

"Because all the nice hotels up north were full," said Cathy.

I whipped out my phone. "Look at this."

"That's a fine old bus," Bernie said appreciatively.

"A fine new bus. It's Malcolm and Angela's new motorhome, presently in the south, but soon to be placed in my care."

"It's very swish," said Cathy.

"I have permission to use it. Do you fancy heading off on a trip in March?"

"Yes," said Bernie.

"We might scratch it," said Cathy.

Bernie snorted scornfully. "Rubbish, I've never scratched a vehicle in my life. Name the day and we'll be ready."

I prodded my phone, as it also possessed a high-tech calendar. "How about… Saturday the 17th of March?" I said, as Easter fell at the end of the month and Inma would have to work in the bar. "We'd better not go for more than a week, as I don't want to abuse their generosity."

"They might want to use it then," said Cathy.

"I'll ask them, and I'll ask Inma. Where shall we go?"

"North," said Bernie.

"South," said Cathy. "It'll still be too cold up north."

"We'll be used to it by then. It's your shout, Alan."

"And Inma's, but I think south is best in March, don't you?"

"Hmm, maybe."

"And as long as we don't scratch it we'll be able to go north another time," I said, wondering when that would be and hoping that Inma was wrong about Malcolm's possible motives for lending me the van, though I was a free agent and he couldn't *oblige* me to do anything I didn't want to do, I hoped.

"South then," said Bernie. "I shan't be planting my olive trees until later in the spring, so I can fit a trip in."

After a leisurely lunch I drove back to the bar and found it almost empty. Inma was talking to an elderly couple, while Randi was seated at the innermost table with a tall, erect man with wavy grey hair and a trim little moustache.

"Is he the one?" I murmured in English when she was pouring my coffee.

She frowned. "He's her friend, yes. Don't stare."

While she continued to chat to the couple I was able to subtly observe the two alleged lovebirds over the old man's shoulder. He seemed to be doing most of the talking, in a voice as clipped as his tash, while Randi gazed into his eyes in a friendly but not especially besotted way. He gesticulated quite a lot, almost as if he were directing traffic, while her hands lay primly crossed on the table. I could hear little of what they said, but it didn't seem like they were planning to elope any time soon. On standing to leave he patted her hand just the once, before almost catching me spying, so briskly did he turn around and march out, looking neither right nor left. I heard his car – presumably the black Mercedes coupé I'd parked next to – give a throaty roar and speed away, upon which Randi stood up, bid us a cheery farewell, and sauntered out.

A minute or so later I decided I needed a breath of fresh air, so I strolled outside and, lo and behold, at the end of the street there was the Mercedes, with two human forms just visible through the small rear window. On heading back inside I crossed paths with the elderly couple and as I strolled insouciantly up to the bar I was met with a stern and slightly ironical look.

"What?" I said.

She slid a small notepad and a pen towards me.

"What?"

"Are you not going to jot down your findings?"

"Oh…"

She chuckled. "You'd never make a private detective."

"What's going on with those two? You never tell me anything."

"Because I'm not a gossip."

"Nor am I, but… but I feel bad for Arvid."

"Rubbish, you don't even like him."

"That's not the point."

"What is the point?"

"Er, I don't know."

"We must live and let live, Alan," she said, looking at her watch.

"Is 5.25 still Juan Antonio's time?"

"Yes."

"Then you've got five minutes to spill the beans."

"To spill what?"

"Er… to tell me what they're up to. I know you won't tell me at home, so tell me now."

She sighed, but didn't grasp my hand as I hoped she might. "It's a free country, Alan, but if you must know, he often comes for coffee, pretends to leave alone, then they drive off somewhere, probably to his chalet, a couple of kilometres from here. That's all there is to tell."

"Who is he?" I said, my eyes mere slits, as I wasn't going to be fobbed off so easily.

She sighed again. "He's called Jaime. He was a captain in the army. He's fifty-two, divorced, is renting a big chalet and has inherited quite a lot of money, or so Juan Antonio says, as he's the only one who has dared to quiz him."

"*Dared* to quiz him?"

"He's quite aloof. He's polite enough, but he rarely speaks to anyone except Randi. I think Juan Antonio got him talking about bullfighting and then began to pry."

"Arvid has guns, you know?"

"He might have some too."

"Ha, then there'll be a gunfight, probably here," I said, before crouching and shooting at her over the bar with appropriate sound effects.

"Been drinking, has he?" said Juan Antonio from the door as I fired my last bullet.

"No, just being childish," she said.

I blew on the barrel and holstered my gun.

"I've just seen his Mercedes on the road," he said.

"Ooh, where were–"

"No! I won't have stupid gossip in my bar," Inma said so fiercely that only I knew, or hoped, that it was an act.

We both mumbled apologies and, while she tidied up, spoke of trivial matters in hushed, chastised tones. When Rosa arrived we set off home.


"Yes, I'm sure Rosa won't mind me having that week off," Inma said when I'd apprised her of our proposed trip to the south.

I didn't mention Randi to her again, and she won't feature for a while, but I assure you there's a reason why I'm keeping you in the loop, in case you think I'm just a chronic busybody.

# 8

Fearful of bogging myself down in a mire of building bulletins, I'm going to speed things along a bit and relate only briefly the events prior to the Hymer's second journey to the south. After their enjoyable trip to the Malaga coast, Malcolm and Angela had yet to set foot in Spain again, taking a February holiday in Cuba instead, as variety is the spice of life, especially if you've got pots of money.

When the Manchegos finished their gruelling six-week stint, the house was well on the way to becoming a hotel. After they'd gone – next stop Benidorm – the plumbers and electricians came in, and Cristóbal's team continued to work eleven-hour shifts, five or six days a week. By the time we set off in the Hymer I was able to tell Malcolm that only an earthquake or the Black Death would prevent them from finishing on time.

"Well make sure that neither of those things happen, Alan," was his droll response.

During a sunny week in late February Juan and I created the steps and patio. I began the job as a mere labourer, but by the end of it I liked to think of myself as a semi-skilled workman, as he'd allowed me to tile half of the patio and even a few steps, under his ever-watchful eye. The railings were easy enough to erect and Inma was delighted with our new rooftop haven which boasted much better views than the yard in front of the cave. As I didn't consider us to be a charitable concern, I broached the subject of payment over a delicious seafood paella that Inma made after the last tile had been laid.

"Pay me? For what? I was just helping out," Juan said, waving a prawn in the air.

"For a whole week. You must accept something," said Inma.

"I'll accept your husband's help next week then, as we're driving to Vitoria and back."

"All right, but that'll be a favour too," I said, waving a mussel shell.

"You're on. I'll pick you up on Monday at six."

"At six? It's not so far, is it?"

He smiled. "We'll take our time. You want to see the north, don't you?"

"Yes, I do."

On Monday we set of in the dark and by sunrise we'd passed Albacete and were eating up the miles towards Madrid.

"When you get tired I'll drive for a bit," I said, but he pressed on for another hour before we stopped to refuel ourselves and the van. I then took the wheel and he navigated the tricky bit around the east of Madrid, after which I suggested a more leisurely break.

"When we get to the north," he said, so I drove on through mostly flat country until he allowed me to pull off the motorway at Aranda del Duero, in the province of Burgos and a little over five hundred kilometres from home.

"It's gone cloudy," I said as I drove along a flat road lined with warehouses.

"That's because we've reached the north. Look how green it is. Aranda will give you a taste of what the north is like."

The blocks of flats on the outskirts were slightly more stylish than those in the south, but it wasn't until we'd crossed the tree-lined River Duero and entered the *casco viejo*, or old town, that I got my first real taste of northern architecture.

"This is the *Plaza Mayor*," he said after guiding me along a strangely quiet street.

"Wow, it's beautiful," I said, marvelling at the old two and three-storey buildings, many with pretty arches, around the large, traffic-free square.

"Most towns and cities in the north have squares like this. You get used to them after a while. Now you'd better reverse, as we're not supposed to be here."

I chose that opportune moment to relinquish the wheel, and before I knew it we were back in the modern suburbs.

"Are we not stopping to look around?"

"Not here. You can always come back another time."

"All right."

"Burgos is too big a place to stop for lunch," he said a while later when the city came into view on the plain. "But if you like Aranda, you'll love it. Great cathedral and… other things."

Conscious that I was on a work trip, I didn't demur, but I did point out that I was rather hungry.

"Me too." He looked at his watch. "We can start to take it easy now. We'll stop at another nice town, on a bigger river."

Thus it was that at three o'clock I found myself finally eating in a cheap restaurant near the fine *Plaza de España* in the town of Miranda del Ebro. Apart from speaking slightly more clearly, the people seemed much the same as down south. I mentioned this to Juan.

"What did you expect?"

"I don't know, but I've read that people are jolly and carefree in the south, and staid and sober in the north."

"Are people jolly and carefree in Vicente's bar?"

"Er, not really. I suppose the south really means Andalucía."

"Hmm, but don't expect to see too many people like your friend Arturo down there either. Folk are much the same everywhere, I've found. It's the greenery and the buildings that are so different in the north, and the weather."

"Yes," I said, looking out at the ominously dark sky.

"I'm surprised it hasn't rained yet. It always rains when I come north, unless it snows, but it's mild today." He knocked back his coffee. "Come on, we'll be in the Basque Country in no time."

No sooner had we crossed the border and reached hillier country than the heavens opened, so it wasn't just the scenery that reminded me of England. I'd hoped to visit the city of Vitoria (Gasteiz to the Basques), but Juan said it was far too busy a place to bother with in the rain, and as his friend lived in a nearby village we'd be better off going straight there. Enrique, Juan's pal, and his Basque wife, Aroa, were friendly and hospitable and she cooked us a tasty stew with broad beans, followed by lamb chops. I'd like to report a joyous evening of sparkling conversation, but Juan and I were tired out after our early start and hit the sack at about ten.

We set off at half past six, in the rain, and loaded the van at a warehouse on the outskirts of Vitoria. The journey back was awful, not so much the dreary motorway trip past Zaragoza and Teruel, which was bad enough, but the endless trundling around the industrial estates of Valencia, Alicante and Murcia, where we dropped off Enrique's goods, before arriving home completely shattered at ten in the evening.

"It's been a long day," I said as I drove up the lane to the hamlet.

"Too long. We should have left Alicante and Murcia for tomorrow, but I'm glad it's done."

I yawned. "Me too."

"What did you think of the north?"

"I like it."

"One needs more time to appreciate it."

"Yes, a lot more."

"There's much to explore up there, though I'm not keen to repeat this trip too soon."

"Me neither, but Inma and I are definitely going north this summer."

"If you have time."

"I will have time. I'll make time," I said, more determined than ever not to get too tied up at the hotel.

"Good trip?" Inma said when I staggered through the door.

"The trip back was hell, but the north is great. We'll have to go this summer."

"Yes. Shall I make you a quick omelette?" she said, perceiving my somnolent state.

"Yes, please."

"Zefe's still here," she said while I ate. "You must take him home tomorrow or he'll start to think that he lives here."

"I will."

# 9

"Don't worry about a thing, Alan. I'll look after the place while you're gone," Zefe said, patting the Hymer's rear-view mirror with his stick.

"Don't do that," I yelped, eager to collect Cathy and Bernie and slip into a rear passenger seat, as he'd promised to drive the great long thing. "Enjoy yourself, but remember that Natalia's coming for a week after we get back," I said, which was a barefaced lie that Inma had insisted I tell him in order to re-establish his weekly two to three-night stays, rather than the five or even six-night residencies that he'd been wangling for a while.

I drove through town at a snail's pace and soon handed Bernie the keys with great relief, as he really is a pro driver and I felt the Hymer would be safer in his hands.

"Where to then?" he said. "I fancy putting this beast through its paces on some mountain roads."

"No, Bernie," Cathy and I said almost simultaneously.

I looked at her.

"I've checked the weather forecast and everywhere inland is almost as cold as here. I think we should go straight to the coast."

Bernie looked at me.

"Yes, I've done a bit of research too and a lot of inland campsites are closed until Easter."

"Campsites? What do we need them for? We can stop wherever we want in this. Up a mountain track, on a street, next to a beach."

I looked pointedly at the gleaming, unblemished silver paintwork. "No, Bern, we can't take any risks. If we scratch it, who knows how Malcolm might react?" I pictured Inma and a scaled down Natalia in a motorboat. "Accepting favours from a boss is a risky business, which is why I want us to drive straight to one of the campsites I've looked into. Once it's parked up I'll feel a lot more relaxed."

"Chicken. Fair enough though. Where to then?"

"Down to Murcia, onto the motorway for a couple of hours, then off it just past Almuñécar. I've seen a campsite that should be all right," I said, my casual tone belying the fact that I'd spent hours on the laptop, studying the safest routes and even – and I kid you not – the width of the campsite gates, as until the Hymer was safely parked and plugged into the mains, I wouldn't begin to enjoy the holiday.

"How far is it?" Bernie asked.

"About four hundred kilometres, mostly motorway."

"Four hours then. Come on, we'll be there for lunch."

"I don't want you to hurry or strain the engine, Bern."

"Ha, this beast's got 180 horsepower." He grinned as he pulled on his tractor driving gloves. "Lock the gate behind us, there's a good lad."

When we got off the track and onto the road I was soon able to relax, as in the passenger seats behind the two swivel chairs up front I felt like I was on a coach, and coach drivers hardly ever crash, unless they're sleepy, and Bernie certainly wasn't, as he prattled on about all the walking, sunbathing and swimming he was going to do.

"It won't be so warm," said Inma. "Remember it is still March."

Cathy swiped her smartphone. "Eighteen degrees in Almuñécar today."

"Too cold to swim," said Inma.

"Ha, you'll see, lass."

"What's the name of the campsite, Alan?" Cathy asked.

I told her.

"Hmm… let's have a look at the reviews."

We soon learnt that the campsite, as well as being one of the best that folk had ever visited, was also one of the worst in Europe.

"Why do people write such different things?" Inma asked.

"Because some people are pillocks," said Bernie. "They find a dirty loo and they can't wait to vent their spleen by writing a bad review. It's a sign of the times. The *power* that folk feel in their fingertips when they get on the computer these days is pathetic. Bloody nobodies who can ruin a business, just like that. It's a good job there weren't computer reviews in my day or I'd have been out on my arse."

I chuckled. "Did you get that, Inma?"

"I think so. What is spleen?"

"El bazo," Cathy said, quick as a flash.

"Yes," I said, though I hadn't known it. "But what is to *vent* one's spleen, Cathy?" I said, as I did know that.

"Er… desahogarse, isn't it?"

"Muy bien, Cathy," I said.

"I understand now," said Inma.

"So what do you all think about these dastardly reviewers, eh?" said Bernie.

"What is dastardly?" Inma asked.

"Bad," said Cathy.

"Yes, or *ruin*, or *vil*, like vile," I said.

"Or pésimo," said Inma. "What did you say, Bernie?"

"Nowt, I'm just the chauffeur."

"What is nowt?" said Inma, and so we went on talking about linguistic matters for the first hour of the journey. I felt bad that Bernie was being left out, but it wouldn't do him any harm to see how far behind he was falling, as Inma's English was also progressing well.

By then, you see – and I feel a lecture coming on, so skip this paragraph if you like – I was more convinced than ever that age isn't the barrier to language learning that many people claim. Although it's certainly easier for young people to learn, there was my sister at the ripe old age of fifty-nine – and without as strong a background in French as I'd had – improving week by week. The hours she spent with her oldies, plus her constant though not excessive studies, had turned her from a non-believer into a person already able to understand most conversations and say what she needed to say. Most middle-aged expats don't learn the language because they think themselves incapable, can't be bothered, or both. If only they set aside an hour a day for study, they'd soon find that it paid off and they'd be able to communicate with the folk in whose country they'd chosen to spend the rest of their lives. Even those who have little time for books, like Bernie, can make great strides if only they try, and personally I believe that those who remain monolingual outsiders in the country of their choice are only living half a life. An hour a day is all it takes. Who can't spare that? Lecture over, sorry.

"There is the road to Águilas," Inma said just after we'd passed Lorca and its towering castle. "You must all come there this summer, to my parents' apartment."

I pictured her father and heard wedding bells.

"Do they not mind that you're living in sin?" said the devilish little mind-reader in the driving seat. I'd told him about her father's hints and he might have been getting his own back after being ignored for so long.

"Living in sin? Ah, yes, I understand. Not really, but they are quite traditional, so I think they will like it if we get married one day."

"Why wait?" said the bald-headed blighter. "We could have a *big* wedding party to celebrate."

"Shut up, Bernie," said my sis.

"After the divorce we will see," Inma said, squeezing my hand. "But it isn't so important to me."

Not *so* important, I thought, and that little word was enough to trigger off one of my not infrequent periods of perturbation, but not for long, as by the time we'd driven into Andalucía I'd made up my mind to ask her to marry me as soon as the divorce papers had been signed. I was almost certain she'd accept and would agree to a nice quiet registry office affair, followed by a party at the cave, paid for by us, as I didn't want Inma's father to think that the offer of the proceeds of his delightful doubloon had influenced our decision, and nor did I want him to part with a family heirloom.

"A penny for your thoughts, Alan," said the lucky lady.

"Oh, just thinking about coins. Are we going to stop for a break soon, Bern?"

"No need."

"I need a pee," I said.

"There's a bog in the bus. I won't swerve, I promise."

"Stop at the next services," Cathy ordered.

"Aye aye, ma'am."

After stretching our legs and breathing in the balmy southern air, we pressed on past the city of Almería and reached the campsite in the coastal village of La Herradura before three o'clock.

"This is all right," said Bernie after he'd parked with precision and jumped out.

"It's a little oasis," said Cathy. "What are these tropical-looking trees?"

"Hay chirimoyas, nísperos y aguacates," said Inma.

Cathy looked at me.

"Er, aguacate is avocado, but I don't know the others in English."

Out came her phone. "Níspero is loquat, whatever that is, and chirimoya is the same, so that's an easy one."

"There's no fruit now, but the trees look nice," I said. "It's a bit of a scruffy place, but it's all right, isn't it?"

Cathy and Inma agreed that it was.

Meanwhile Bernie was back in the van and soon appeared dressed only in swim shorts.

"I'm going for my daily swim now."

"It will be too cold," said Inma.

"We're going to have lunch," said Cathy.

"I won't be long. Are you man enough to come, Alan?"

I looked up at the sun and said that I was. "It'll cool down soon, so we'd better make the most of it."

So it was that after making some sandwiches we all headed out of the site and down the short street to the rather stony beach, where a few people were sitting in various stages of undress. One woman was paddling, but none were swimming, so it was with some trepidation that I followed Bernie into the sea. Bernie marched straight in and let out a whoop, presumably of joy, after launching himself into the gentle waves. I entered more gingerly and would probably have chickened out at thigh height had he not been treading water and grinning fiendishly at me, so I plunged in and boy was it cold, but I swam grimly out until I was by his side.

"You get used to it after a while," he said, panting like an ageing bulldog.

"Yes, it's not so bad once you're in," I lied.

"Might as well swim for a bit while we're at it," he stammered.

"Yes, work up an appetite," I gasped, before commencing a frantic breaststroke parallel to the beach. Bernie doggie paddled doggedly by my side and after about thirty yards he said that we oughtn't to overdo it on the first day and I promptly agreed, despite having swum many lengths in the municipal pool that winter.

"I enjoyed that," Bernie said when we'd floundered out.

"Yes, a bit bracing, but very pleasant."

"We could jog for a bit now."

"Yes, let's," I said, and although Bernie probably hadn't jogged since leaving school, and I hadn't for a while, we found it to be just the thing for restoring the blood flow to our benumbed limbs, so when we returned to the girls a few minutes later we were both winded but a little warmer.

"That was nice," said Bernie.

"You're both mad," said Cathy, who had rolled up her sleeves.

"Dry yourselves," said Inma, who hadn't even bothered to do that, as a keen breeze was making things none too warm.

"This beach isn't very comfortable," Cathy said as we ate our butties.

"We'll buy some mats," said Bernie, still shivering sporadically.

"I think it isn't warm enough for a beach holiday," said Inma, who later told me that she couldn't remember ever sitting on a beach before June.

"We'll have to find other things to do," said Cathy, reaching for her phone.

"We can drive the Hymer up into the hills," said Bernie, and on seeing my downcast expression, "Or hire a car."

"We can catch a bus to Almuñécar," I said.

"And other places from there," said Cathy, swiping away.

"We can go for walks," said Inma.

"Yes, up that headland, or the one over there," Cathy said, as La Herradura is situated in a wide bay.

"There are lots of things to do," I said as I watched a little dog enter the sea up to its knees and come scurrying out.

"As long as I have time for a quick swim every day," said Bernie, the third of a bottle of wine he'd just knocked back giving him Dutch courage, no doubt.

Later on, well wrapped up, we strolled along the seafront and had dinner at one of the many restaurants in the resort whose development had been modest due to the mediocre beach, I believe, but this suited us just fine. We spoke English most of the time, but occasionally switched to Spanish to give Inma's brain a rest, and we all looked forward to the coming days.

"If Alan wasn't so fussy about the van, I'd be tempted to move on to somewhere else soon, but I'm sure we'll keep ourselves occupied," said Bernie over coffee.

"There's plenty to do," said Cathy, tapping her oracle.

"You could always buy a camper van, Bern," I said.

"Don't give him ideas, Alan."

"Hmm," said Bernie, tracing something very much like a camper van on the paper tablecloth. "I suppose there are some nice old ones out there."

Cathy groaned and gave me an aggrieved glance.

"Sorry."

"Wait to see if you enjoy this holiday first," said Inma. "It isn't good to buy things for no good reason."

Cathy gave her a grateful glance.

"If I ever got one, it'd be one that I wasn't too worried about scratching," I said.

Both ladies raised their brows.

"But we ought to see how we enjoy this holiday first," I added.

The next day, after we'd all slept fairly well – Cathy and Bernie in the bed at the back, and Inma and I on the cleverly converted sofa bed up front – we had breakfast then headed off on our first exploratory walk to the west. After plodding up through a fairly tasteful housing estate, we emerged onto the scantily wooded headland with splendid panoramic views. After inspecting an old watchtower we followed a path from where we soon spied an isolated beach down below.

"Shall we go there, or will it be too far for you?" I said.

"Ha," said Cathy, before leading the way to a lane which wound its way down to the pebbly beach, where Bernie was amused to see a mixed group of naked, middle-aged people, possibly Germans, by the look of their purple skin and light hair.

"If I'd brought a towel, I'd get bollock naked like them and go for a swim," he said.

"You don't need to swim, Bern. They aren't swimming. Just strip off and let it all hang out."

"I'll hold your clothes," said Cathy.

"Nah, I might get a… aroused."

"Unless Inma strips too, I don't think there's much to arouse you here," she said, as the ladies in the group were pretty flaccid, I must say, without wishing it go into too much detail.

Bernie turned to me. "I dare you."

"Not today, Bern."

Seizing his chance to outdo me, he tore off his t-shirt and shorts, then hesitated with his thumbs hooked under his blue y-fronts.

Cathy hooted with laughter. "You can't go back now. Pull 'em down."

He turned away from us, pulled 'em down, then set off jogging along the beach in his trainers, seeming keen to get away from us and the true nudists.

"How white his bum looks," said Cathy.

"He's going a long way," Inma said as he approached the end of the otherwise deserted beach.

"He's realised the enormity of his act and is now embarrassed to turn back," I said.

"There's no enormity there, worse luck," said Cathy.

"I will go to that restaurant, so he won't be embarrassed," said Inma.

"No, stay here, unless you really can't face it," she said.

"All right. Look, he's coming back now and running in a strange way."

What Bernie was doing was so amusing that I grabbed Inma's phone, determined to immortalise his curious running style, because rather than letting his willy joggle about, or firmly holding it in place and out of sight, he held his right hand about a foot from his body, trying and failing to obscure it from view. While Cathy held up his undies as an incitement to end his ordeal, I snapped merrily away, and it was only after long deliberation that I decided not to use the best of those shots as the cover photo for this book, instead choosing another seaside one to remind me of the trip.

As he approached, walking now and trying to look nonchalant, Inma considerately kneeled down to adjust her shoelace, and Bernie was back in his y-fronts in three seconds flat.

"Flipping heck, I never thought I'd feel so embarrassed," he said, scratching his head. "But it just didn't feel right."

"Nudism is all very well, but I guess there's a reason why we've covered our privates ever since human communities were formed," I said sagely.

"Put on the rest of your clothes," said Cathy.

"I feel fine in my undies, so Alan's probably right. Yes, it's them who're weird," he said, jerking his thumb over his shoulder. "Did they laugh at me?"

"No," said Inma. "They looked serious and some shook their heads."

"They probably are Germans then," I said.

"Racist," said Cathy.

"Or Dutch. Come on, let's get something to eat."

After a light lunch we headed back and reached the Hymer somewhat tired but happy to have completed the slightly strenuous walk.

"While we have a rest, you can go for your daily swim, boys," said Cathy.

"No, I'm not doing any more dares," said Bernie.

"I'll go for a shower instead," I said.

"But we'll swim again before we leave."

"Definitely."

# 10

The following day we caught the bus into Almuñécar, a sizeable town about five miles along the coast to the east. Being March it wasn't too busy and we strolled around the pleasant streets before taking a look at the *Castillo de San Miguel*, which is said to have existed in one form or another since the first century BC. It looked pretty new to me – even Cristóbal would have been impressed by the pointing and rendering – but we found it quite atmospheric and the little museum was interesting.

"This is a nice town," Bernie said during lunch at a seafront restaurant. "But I can't help feeling that we ought to move on soon."

"Why?" said Cathy.

"Because... oh, I guess it's just wanderlust."

"Since when did that condition afflict you? Back home you can scarcely be bothered to go into town," she said.

"It's different at home. There I'm tied to the soil, or soon will be. Now that I'm on the road I feel different."

"Do you not go to the Brit bar anymore?" I asked, wishing to avoid the subject of onward travel.

"Not often. I don't feel like I'm part of that scene now. I prefer going to your bar, Inma, to chew the fat with the locals."

"Thanks, and now I know that you don't mean the food."

"Denise keeps me up to date with the expat news," said Cathy.

"And you tell me," said Bernie.

"Hmm, I suppose we aren't doing much to find new house buyers though, are we?" I said.

"I thought you'd given that up," he said.

I pictured the depleted cornflakes box. I was due another good payday when the hotel was completed, but after that, what?

"Oh, I'm not averse to helping folk to find a nice home. It's better they come to us than go to unscrupulous people."

"Like Juanca," said Inma.

"He's no worse than others," I said.

Bernie asked me if I'd heard from the tireless property trafficker.

"No, not a word since that day at the notary's. He's miffed about being cut out of the hotel building business, but if I go along with a new buyer he'll greet me like a long-lost brother, no doubt. Someone will appear one of these days, I'm sure," I said, reminding myself that I was set to earn some sort of salary at the hotel.

"Yes, they will," said Bernie, before clapping, just the once. "So, are we off somewhere else tomorrow then?"

I groaned silently.

"We're going to Lentegí," said Cathy.

"Where's that?" he asked.

"You'll find out tomorrow."

"And how will we get there?" I said.

"Don't worry. The Hymer will be staying put."

When a white taxi rolled into the campsite the next morning at ten it turned out to be for us. Cathy ushered us in and we were soon speeding along the sinuous main road towards Almuñécar, where the bearded young driver headed inland and we began to climb past verdant orchards, before dipping under the motorway –

impressively raised on huge concrete pillars at this point – and onwards and upwards.

"Are we going far, Cathy?" I asked.

"No, not far. Don't worry, this is on me."

"Not so expensive," said the driver, tapping the taximeter which was clicking merrily away.

On spotting a village up ahead I grasped my knapsack, but we drove straight through it.

"I can feel the air getting thinner," said Bernie, grasping his throat.

On seeing another village up ahead, I tightened my laces, but we drove through and then turned sharp right.

"Look, there's a sign to Lentegí," Inma cried, grasping my hand in anticipation of the delights in store for us in such a far-flung, or high-flung, place.

After several sharp hairpin bends we reached the white village perched on the mountainside and the taxi pulled up beside the remarkably pretty little village hall.

"Gracias," said Cathy, before paying the man.

"You want me to wait?"

"No, gracias."

"No more bus today."

"I know," she said in Spanish. "Adiós."

After he'd turned around and whizzed off, Cathy led us purposefully up the deserted street.

"I bet this place didn't even have a proper road before the advent of tourism," I said.

"Probably not," said Inma. "It's very isolated."

"Why have we come?" Bernie asked.

"Because it's the most remote village I could find, without going too far. To be honest I expected it to be more traditional," she said, pointing at a plush house with a BMW on the drive. "But

I guess us foreigners get everywhere these days. Never mind, let's find somewhere to have a coffee."

When we wandered up a street too narrow for cars to park, I began to get a feel for the place as it once must have been and I was glad we'd come, but after strolling around for twenty minutes we still hadn't found a bar or any other signs of commerce. Though the views of the valley below and the mountains further inland were spectacular, I think the three of us were wondering why Cathy hadn't done her homework.

"I just assumed there'd be at least a bar or a shop," she said when we found ourselves outside the village hall again. "It's got three hundred and odd inhabitants, after all."

"Maybe it's like a lot of small villages in England, where everybody has cars," I ventured, as of the three people we'd seen, two had looked foreign and one old man had puttered past in an old Renault 5.

"Ah, a sign of the times," said Bernie, glancing warily at his wife. "What shall we do now?"

"I'd planned to spend some time here, then walk down to the next village, so I guess we might as well set off now," she said, annoyed that her mystery destination had been a slight disappointment.

She'd warned us to wear stout footwear, however, so it was no great effort to cover the three miles down the deserted road, feeling the benign sun, breathing in the cool air, and marvelling at the views. By the time we reached the larger village of Otivar we all felt invigorated by the walk and ready for a drink. After a brief exploration of its quaint narrow streets, we found a little bar.

"Ah, I've been looking forward to for this," Bernie said when his tankard of beer arrived.

The rest of us had ordered red wine and *casera*, or lemonade. I'd just added a dash of wine when my phone rang.

"Probably Cristóbal," I said, sitting up straighter in my chair. "Ooh, no, it's Beth."

"Probably got a buyer for you," said Bernie, rubbing his hands together.

"For us. Hello, Beth. How are you?"

"Hi, Alan, I'm fine. I'm just calling to tell you that Bill died yesterday. His daughter called me this morning."

"Oh, dear." With all eyes upon me I stood up and went outside. "I'm sorry to hear that."

"Yes, it's sad, but she said he died peacefully and had been happy back home, so… well, I suppose he did have a good innings."

"Yes, I'm… will you go to the funeral?"

"Yes, my husband's away working, so I'll go. I knew his daughter quite well, so I ought to."

"Yes. I'm on holiday in the south now," I said, wondering if I ought to go too.

"That's nice. I guess you won't be going, seeing as you only knew him," she said, and I was grateful for her bluntness, as I really didn't fancy a trip to England just to stand among strangers, apart from Beth, of course.

"No, if I were at home… but no. He was a nice man, wasn't he?"

"A lovely chap, but lonely here in Spain. Folk can stay too long sometimes, and his heart never really left England. I'm glad he went back really."

"Yes. How sad though."

"Yes, it is. Anyway, enjoy the rest of your holiday."

"Yes, thanks."

"I'm still on the lookout for buyers, by the way."

"Oh, yes, good, thanks."

"I'll be in touch."

"Thanks for calling, Beth."

"See you later."

"Bye, Beth."

The news saddened our little party.

"He was a nice old man," said Cathy after a moment's silence.

"A noble man," said Inma.

"Yes, a sound bloke, despite being so posh," said Bernie. "Did Beth mention… er, buyers at all?"

"Bernie! Have some respect," Cathy hissed.

He shrugged. "Life goes on, love."

"She said she was still looking out for them," I mumbled. "I don't know if I ought to go to the funeral."

"Go if you like," said Inma.

"Though you didn't know him *that* well," said Cathy, her practical side reasserting itself.

"And we are on holiday," said Bernie.

"I told Beth that. No, I don't think I'll go. I prefer to remember him as we last saw him, cheerful and looking forward to going home."

"He enjoyed a few months there," said Cathy. "Shame he didn't see one more English spring."

"There's not much point us going to England this summer then. Visiting Bill was the main reason for going, wasn't it?" Bernie said hopefully.

"Hmm," said Cathy, and Bernie was wise enough not to press her on the subject, as I think she knew that visiting his sister and our old Auntie Maud again wasn't a great incentive to repeat last summer's trip when there was so much of Spain still to explore.

She took out her phone and perused it for a while. "Who's up for walking down to the next village for lunch? It's only about two miles."

"I am," said Inma.

"Great," said I.

"We're not going to end up walking *all* the way back, are we?" Bernie moaned.

"No, dear, we'll get the bus from there."

Although there was a bit more traffic on the second leg of our downhill hike, it was pleasant all the same, and between us we identified mango, avocado, pear and loquat trees. The area is known as the *Costa Tropical*, due to its subtropical microclimate, and I asked Bernie if he wouldn't rather live and farm somewhere like it.

"No, all these trees are foreign imports, except maybe the pear trees. I'll stick to my olive trees, like we've done since Roman times."

"It would be nice to live nearer to the sea, I sometimes think," said Inma.

"Would it?" I said, surprised.

"When we retire, I mean. Here, for example, you can be at the beach in a short time."

"Too many foreigners around for my liking. Give me the peace and quiet of the countryside anytime," said Bernie. "Though I'm glad I'm here now," he added after a pause.

"It's very windswept where we live, and much colder in winter than I expected," said Cathy as we reached the first houses of the village of Jete. "Never say never is what I say."

"I'm not going to plant millennial olive trees and then abandon them," Bernie whined.

"They won't be millennial for a while," I said, amused by his attitude, which had changed a heck of a lot in the year since we'd arrived in Spain.

Jete was pretty too, if a little more bustling, and after lunch we boarded the first of two buses back to the campsite.

"You know, if you'd told me we'd be bussing it on this holiday I'd have said, pull the other one, but I'm quite enjoying it," Bernie said after bagging the back seats for us.

"How long is it since you were on a bus?" I said.

"A day."

"No, I mean before that."

"Oof, thirty or forty years, I suppose. I like it though. It's good to watch the locals going about their business."

"Half of them are foreigners," I murmured.

"Yes, well, they are here, but I wouldn't rule out bussing it around other parts of Spain one day."

"I'm glad you like it, because we're bussing it tomorrow as well," said Cathy. "If we all agree, of course."

For the next two days buses became our principal form of transport. The temperature had fallen well below twenty degrees and it was quite cloudy most of the time, so we were happy to travel west to Nerja one day and east to Salobreña the next, but I won't bore you with the details of those busy towns, save to say that Nerja is much more touristy and has lovely beaches and promenades, while Salobreña is more down to earth and set back from the sea, while its beaches are as dark and rough as that of La Herradura.

"I've enjoyed it so far," Bernie said that evening as we ate dinner in the Hymer, having decided to use the cooker at least once.

We concurred that despite the middling to poor weather, we were making the most of our time in the south.

He raised his fork and waved it about.

"Eat that mushroom first," said Cathy.

He cleared the fork and waved it again. "But I do think, if you're all agreeable, that we ought to go somewhere else on our way home."

"Why?" said Cathy.

"Well, we've sort of done this area now, and as it's not beach weather, even for a tough guy like me, I think we should make tracks and go home by a different route."

I moved my head from side to side in the noncommittal Spanish way.

"If we just drive straight back on the motorway it won't really have been a motorhome tour at all, will it?"

Cathy consulted her phone. "Going inland via Granada is a recommended route too."

"No way are we taking the Hymer into a big city like that," I said anxiously. "I'm sorry, but we can go there another time in the car."

"The route is nice though, and the roads are good," said Inma. "We could go that way and stop somewhere quiet for a night or two."

"The campsites might still be closed," I said feebly.

Bernie slapped the table. "Oh, come on, Alan. This thing's got everything we need. We can stop anywhere we like out in the wilds. This isn't England, you know. There's *space* here. I mean, we've hardly even used the loo yet."

"Not for number twos," said Cathy.

"And we'll have to clean the thing from top to bottom anyway, so we might as well get some use out of it," said the persuasive one, sensing that he was nearing a breakthrough.

"And we're supposed to check out tomorrow, though we can stay if we want," said Cathy.

I nibbled a bit of chicken and nodded slowly. "All right. We'll go back via Granada, but we won't stop for the night anywhere that's not safe."

"Great," said Bernie.

"And we won't enter any town centres. They might have narrow streets or unforeseen obstacles."

"I haven't scratched a vehicle in my life, but all right."

"That's settled then," said Cathy. "All that remains is for you two to have that final swim that you promised yourselves."

Bernie and I agreed to forsake that pleasure in order to make an early start.

"I'm not sure about this," I said at half past seven the following evening as the sky reddened to the west.

"We'll be as safe as houses here," Bernie said.

"It will be dark soon," said Inma.

"It's big enough anyway," said Cathy, scuffing her shoe on the dusty earth.

"I suppose it's better than going on in the dark," I conceded, as the flat patch of land beside the road on the outskirts of Huéscar, in the far north of the province of Granada, was the best we'd seen for a while. After driving up from the coast and admiring Granada and its Alhambra Palace from the bypass, we'd climbed onto the plateau and stopped at the town of Guadix. There we'd visited the baroque cathedral, the lovingly restored *alcazaba*, or Arab fortress, and made a brief foray into the *Barrio de Cuevas*, where Inma and I were able to compare our cave house to a neighbourhood full of them, ranging from dwellings carved into the solid rock to a few extremely crumbly affairs where I'd have been even more nervous about spending the night than where we ended up.

In the end it was a good experience, as few cars passed and no-one bothered us at all. It was a starry night and as we sat outside, well wrapped up against the cold at about a thousand metres above sea level, we marvelled at the vastness of it all.

"This is the way to go in a motorhome," said Bernie, mellowed by the wine he'd drunk. "Like hoboes, stopping wherever we want and without a care in the world."

I glanced at the Hymer. "Hardly hoboes, Bern."

"Who needs campsites when the whole of Spain is our oyster, eh?"

"Not in this though. I don't think I'm going to ask to borrow it again. I'm just too nervous about damaging it."

"We've noticed that," said Cathy.

"Hey, we could buy one for the four of us. You know, share it."

"One of these?" said Inma, looking startled.

"No, nothing like this beast. Just a camper van."

"What, pre-war?" said Cathy.

"No, we'd have to be practical. Even those old VW campers are too small for us really."

"First we should go away in the car and take tents," said Inma.

"Tents?" said Bernie, clearly unimpressed.

Inma switched to slow Spanish. "Why not? It's the same principle and if we enjoyed a camping trip, we could think about getting a camper van. One can stay in hotels too, of course. I don't believe in buying expensive things on a whim. One should be sure that it's the right thing to do before spending all that money."

"Did you get that, Bern?"

"Sure did. How do you say 'dampers' in Spanish?"

"In that context, I don't know, but Inma's right. I mean, how much use will Malcolm and Angela get out of this thing?"

"They can afford it, but it's a big expense for us, as I'm not having some clapped out pile of junk. Let's forget about it for now," said Cathy.

"And look at the stars," said Inma.

We looked at the stars.

"This is the life," said Bernie, who could never keep quiet for long. "We could do this again tomorrow night, nearer to home."

"If we find a place as big and safe and quiet as this, yes," I said, still fearing that a stray pyromaniac might burn us in our beds, something that seldom happens on campsites.

We soon turned in and spent a peaceful night.

The following morning we awoke to hear rain hammering on the roof, so in true hobo style we filled the tank at the next petrol station and drove the 180 kilometres back to Cathy and Bernie's place where, after consulting Angela, we left the Hymer, as it would be safer there than at the isolated hotel.

"I suppose in a way we chickened out a bit today," I said to Bernie as he drove us home in the sunshine.

"Yes, but we've seen a lot, haven't we? Did you enjoy it, Inma?"

"Very much. I've enjoyed travelling with you and Cathy."

"So have we, with you two. When's our next expedition then?"

"Who knows? What with the hotel and everything… oh, aren't Christine and co. coming sometime soon?" I asked.

"Not till the summer was the last I heard."

"Oh, well, that's good. I should have more time then."

"You hope," said Inma.

"I hope."

# 11

"Álvaro said he didn't see Inma's daughter once," Zefe said peevishly a few days after our return.

"She was studying. She hardly ever left the annex."

"He saw no movement there whatsoever."

"Unless she came to study in the cave, for a change," I said, the blood rising to my face, as I'm a poor liar, not having practised the art much since my schooldays.

This conversation was taking place in the municipal swimming pool, at the shallow end of our usual lane where we were resting prior to tackling our final lengths.

"Did Álvaro not come to see you in town?"

"Of course, and he admired the new floor."

"Good."

"Although he noticed a few loose tiles in the bathroom."

I sighed. "I've told you I'll come to stick all the loose ones down when I can," I said, having been spending much more time at the hotel, supervising the laying of the lawns which Angela had ordered, and personally clearing the undergrowth from beneath the nine weary pine trees where three wooden benches were soon to be placed. Being there in work clothes made me more inclined to spend time with the builders, the number of whom appeared to be dwindling day by day.

"Where's Diego?" I asked Arturo one sunny afternoon after wiping the sweat from my brow.

"Gone."

"I can see that. Where's he gone?"

"To a new job."

"What? You can't start a new job until you've finished this one."

"Tell Cristóbal that."

"I will. Where is he?"

"Upstairs."

"With Miguel?" I asked, as they often worked together on the trickiest jobs.

"No, Miguel's gone too."

"Right," I said, before stomping upstairs like Basil Fawlty on the trail of Manuel, as my legs are pretty long too.

When I came across Cristóbal, however, just the sight of his stocky legs on the end of a stepladder dissuaded me from taking him to task.

"Er, have you got a minute, Cristóbal?"

"Can't you see I'm busy?" he said in a muffled voice, his upper half being out of sight through a bathroom ceiling panel.

"Yes, but I want a word... please."

He took his time climbing down. "Well?"

"Why have Diego and Miguel gone to do another job?" I asked boldly.

"Because it came up, and I can't afford to turn down work. If you'd done *your* job and persuaded them to have a house built, we'd have moved straight onto that, but as things stand I have to think about the future."

"But what about the deadline?"

"What about it?"

"There's still a lot to do here."

"It'll be done in time, all being well."

My peeved pout turned into a cunning smile. "Remember your contract, Cristóbal. If you finish late, you'll pay for it."

"I haven't forgotten, and *we* would pay for it. Anyway, if you're so concerned, why don't you stop messing about outside and lend a hand in here?"

"Me?"

"Who else? Arturo can show you how to mix and that'll free him up to do other jobs."

"I know how to mix," I snapped. "And lay tiles and… things."

"Well get him to show you how he mixes, then send him up here."

"It's already four o'clock."

He grinned. "We don't finish until seven."

I went downstairs to learn how to mix sand and cement the way Cristóbal liked it.

That evening when I was laying out my overalls for the following day's early start, my phone rang.

"Hello, Angela," I said, unsure whether or not to tell her that I was going to join her manual workforce.

"Alan, we must recruit right away," she said with uncharacteristic urgency.

"I thought you were coming in a week or so to do that."

"Malcolm's just reminded me that workers have to give a month's notice, in Britain at least. In any case it's time to start looking for staff."

"Yes, I think it is," I said, smiling at my overalls. It wasn't that I was unwilling to lend a hand on the job, but Cristóbal had assumed I'd be doing eleven-hour shifts every day like the others and I found the prospect a bit daunting.

"I'm flying out tomorrow morning, as there isn't a moment to lose."

"Right, well I'll drive the Hymer over to the hotel then. Is Malcolm not coming too?"

"No, he's busy. Er, Alan, I'm not too keen on staying in the Hymer alone."

"Right."

"Or on hiring a car and driving alone."

"Right. Well I'll pick you up at the airport then."

"Thank you, Alan."

"Would you like to stay here with us? We have a little annex for guests," I said, Zefe's irate face flashing before my eyes.

"Yes, please, I'd like that. I'm not used to travelling alone, you see."

She told me her arrival time and we said adios until the morrow.

"We can't possibly put her in the annex," Inma said when I told her the news. "She must eat and sleep here with us. We do have spare rooms, remember."

"You don't mind, do you?"

"Not at all. She's a nice lady and it'll be good for you to spend time with her without that huge husband of hers."

"Yes."


When Angela and I arrived home from the airport at noon the next day, she slid her laptop from its case and we got down to work.

"I've found a good job site, so I think we'll advertise on it," she said, showing me the list of jobs.

"OK."

"Cristóbal tells me that we now have the permits, but it's all ever so complicated. Oh, we shouldn't have gone to Iceland to see the northern lights. I should have been here."

I chuckled politely. "You do travel a lot."

"There'll be no more holidays for a while now. We're going to have a lot of work to do."

"Yes," I said, not sure whether or not to be pleased by her use of the word 'we'. Although it made me feel wanted, it might also herald future irksome ties, but I decided to go with the flow for the time being.

While I made a pot of tea she studied the job website, her Spanish by now being good enough to understand that sort of thing.

"We can either use an agency or advertise the jobs ourselves," she said.

"The agencies are the experts," I said. "I mean, I'm not even sure what staff we need, and we do need to appear to be professional."

"True, but I want us to interview the candidates."

"Of course."

Anyway, to cut a dull story short, after contacting an employment agency based in Elda we drove over to see their resident hotel expert, who recommended that we employ a manager, an assistant manager, three receptionists cum administrators, two cooks, three kitchen assistants, four waiters and/or waitresses, three chambermaids, a caretaker cum maintenance man, and a gardener cum chauffeur, the two final posts being of a flexible nature.

"That should do for a start," said the placid, balding young man in English, which I didn't mind because Angela had to understand every word. "There are only twelve rooms, after all."

"Er, that seems like rather a lot of staff," I said, as Angela appeared to have been struck dumb.

He peered at me patiently over his slim reading glasses. "They will have time off, days off and holidays, remember."

"Ah, yes."

"Some of them may be part-time," he conceded. "I suggest you give six-month contracts to begin with for most of the posts. That way if they're no good you can get rid of them after a month."

"We'll do that then," said Angela. "We want to have all those people you mentioned, and we'll pay about ten percent over the normal rates."

The man smiled. "Good. The only problem I foresee is finding a good manager at such short notice. You should have come to us earlier," he said, looking accusingly at me.

"I am the owner," said the owner. "Alan here is a friend who is assisting me."

I breathed one of my inaudible sighs of relief.

"I see. A good manager would normally give more notice to his employer, as it is a key post. Ideally you would already have a manager to carry out the interviews, as an experienced manager would know which people are right for each post."

"How can we get a manager quickly?" Angela asked.

"By offering them a high salary and a good contract, of course."

"I'll do that," she said. "But won't they have to give notice anyway?"

He smiled, showing his teeth this time. "If offered a high enough salary and a permanent contract they may be persuaded to leave their employer quickly. The hotel world is like that."

"Then there's no time to lose," she said. "Please find me candidates for all the jobs as soon as possible."

"Of course. Leave it with me. Do you wish to interview them here, with our expert assistance, or at the hotel?"

"Here," I said.

"At the hotel," she said.

"At the hotel," I confirmed.

"I want them to see the place and where it is."

"Where is it?" he asked.

I described the location.

"Hmm, most of the staff will be local people, but they must have their own transport. The manager, however, will probably come from further away, possibly the coast, so you may have to offer accommodation at first, to… entice him to come."

"Or her. We'll do that," said Angela.

Impressed by the man's English, which was at least as good as my Spanish, notwithstanding his rotten accent, I asked him to recommend a really good *asesoría*, or advisory service, to help manage the business. I suppose I should have run this past Angela first, but on grasping the magnitude of the forthcoming venture I wanted it to go as smoothly as possible, not least because the thought of becoming involved in such unfamiliar affairs made my hair curl. I mean, my dealings with bureaucracy in England had been minimal and I wasn't about to become embroiled in something that I might struggle to get out of if I didn't like it. In short, the old, responsibility-free me was reasserting himself before it was too late.

He handed Angela a card. "These *asesores* are the best in the area and their offices are just down the street. We work with them a lot and they are familiar with the hotel trade. Tell them I sent you. They will assign you a person who speaks excellent English."

"We'll go there now," said Angela.

I could have kissed her, but restrained myself.

It was six o'clock by the time we left Elda and I hummed softly as I piloted the Ibiza along the mainly straight road back to town.

"You sound happy, Alan," Angela said with a chuckle.

"I feel relieved. It all sounds much simpler now that you've left so many things in the hands of experts."

"I knew we had to really, as Malcolm told me what I must do."

"Ah, right."

"I realise that you don't want to get involved in the management of the hotel, Alan, so don't worry about it. You're being a great help anyway, looking after me and giving me moral support. I'm very grateful for that."

Having felt a bit guilty about being so eager to avoid taking on new responsibilities, I'd totally forgotten that what I was doing was pretty useful too.

"I hope I don't tie you up too much during the coming days, Alan."

I pictured my still clean overalls. "Oh, not at all. I had nothing important to do. I'm more than happy to help."

"You're a good man to have around, Alan."

"Oh, I try to be," I said modestly.


"What time do you call this?" Cristóbal growled the following morning at nine. "And what the hell are you doing dressed like that?"

I just smiled like Clark Gable and surveyed the almost completed reception area, glad that he was there.

"Oh, hello, Angela. I not know you here," said the great chump a moment later.

"Does he often speak to you like that?" she muttered.

"Oh, we like to tease each other. I'd been planning to lend a hand today, just for fun, you know."

"Hmm. Cristóbal, please show me around."

After a ten-minute tour we returned to reception and Angela said she'd only seen two men on the job.

"Yes, and me," he said, displaying his dusty hands.

"There were lots of men here the last time I came. Where are they now?"

"Manchegos finish. Also plumbers and electrical men finish, more or less."

"And your other men?"

"Not here today."

"But there are still many things to do."

"Yes, no problem."

"The final deadline is the end of April. It would be good to have it finished before then, as the furniture and everything else will be arriving the week before."

"Yes, no problem."

She nodded and clicked her tongue ominously. "Malcolm will call you later. Come on, Alan."

I gave Cristóbal a pitying look and followed her into the future lounge, before borrowing Arturo and fetching a half-decent table and the best four chairs we could find.

She surveyed the freshly plastered but unpainted walls and sighed. "I suppose this will have to do for the interviews."

"Yes, at least they'll see that it's a brand new hotel that they're going to become involved in," I said, feeling more upbeat in my role as a mere friend and helper.

"As soon as we get applicants I want us to interview them, Alan. They'll be the keen ones and if they're all right I'll take them on."

"OK."

"I hope I'm not imposing myself on you. I can go to the hotel in town, if you like, as I suppose I'll be here for at least a week."

"No, you're more than welcome to stay with us," I said, as the evening before she'd proved herself to be a charming, discreet guest with whom we both got on well.

"And we must talk about your salary soon. You've already started work, after all."

I held up my hand and shook my head. "No, Angela, not until the hotel opens," I said magnanimously on recalling the whopping great commission that Juanca and I had received. "Until then I'm just a friend lending a hand."

"I don't know what I'd do without you."

I shrugged and smiled bashfully, before opening the unvarnished door and ushering her out.

# 12

By that evening the agency had forwarded the CVs of thirteen people. Five of them were locals and I helped Angela with the wording of an email which asked three of them to present themselves at the hotel the following morning at half-hourly intervals from ten o'clock. I included a link to a map, before asking her if the email wasn't a bit too brief and inflexible.

"No, they're free to reply and ask to come another time, of course, but being a Saturday they should be free. What do you think of the two applicants for the manager's job?"

"Well, the one in Cuba probably won't be able to come quickly enough, but the chap working in Almansa ought to be able to make it all right. It's only thirty-odd miles to the north of here."

"Hmm, I like the fact that he used to work in London and Preston, as his English should be good. Aren't you from near Preston?"

"Quite near, yes."

"But I don't like the gap in his CV, or the fact that he's now managing what appears to be little more than a bed and breakfast. I ask myself what he was doing for a year and a half between his time in Preston and Almansa."

"Hmm, he worked in good hotels in Madrid and London before going to Preston. Shall we see him anyway?"

"We might as well, but let's ask him to come on Monday." She chuckled. "I'd like to get some practice doing tomorrow's interviews first."

She sent him a short email and closed the laptop. "That's enough work for now. I don't want to bore Inma."

She and Inma got on really well and we spoke mostly Spanish, though Angela switched to English when she got stuck or tired. She also retired to her room in the depths of the cave nice and early, so her stay was working out just fine.

"She's a pleasant lady, but I don't really know why she wants to undertake this hotel project when she already has a lot of money," Inma said later in bed. "She must be over sixty, after all."

"Once it's all up and running I think she'll concentrate on her courses. I think that's what really interests her."

"And what do you think you'll do?"

"I don't know. Maybe I'd like to get involved in the courses too. I think the hotel will be just a grind, but the courses might be fun." I yawned. "Time will tell."

"Yes. Oh, Bernie finally got his field ploughed today, so he'll be able to plough it himself from now on. He was in the bar this afternoon with his tractor-driving friend."

"That's good. I'll go over soon." I propped myself on my elbow and gazed into her eyes. "How's Randi, by the way?"

"She's fine. Goodnight."

"Goodnight, love."


After driving through the fog we reached the hotel at nine the next morning and I wasn't altogether surprised to see both of Cristóbal's vans there, not after his 'chat' with Malcolm, but I hadn't expected to see a painters' van too, or an estate car belonging to his plumber friend.

"Buenos días, Cristóbal," I said cheerfully when I found him in the kitchen with said plumber.

"Hola, Alan. It's nice to see you."

I blinked three or four times. "We have interviews today." I patted my document case. "Things are busier here, I see," I said mildly, not wishing to gloat.

"Things are just as I planned them to be," he said softly, perchance chastised by the bollocking he must have received from the big man.

I bet, I thought. "I see," I said. "We will be interviewing in the lounge and won't wish to be disturbed."

He grinned malevolently, suddenly his old self again. "Tell the painters that."

Angela soon told the two painters to apply their pastel tones elsewhere, and after giving the room a quick sweep we were soon ready to begin.

"I feel like I'm the one who's going to be interviewed," I said as I paced around.

"Ha, me too. This is new to both of us, but Malcolm has given me a few tips," she said, before running through the questions that she wanted me to ask, her Spanish being a bit hesitant for such a task.

The first applicant arrived at two minutes to ten. The tallish young man had whizzed up the drive in an old Ford Fiesta and trotted inside.

"I recognise him from a restaurant in town," I said from the window.

"Is he a good worker?"

"He seemed to be."

The youngster introduced himself as Fran. He wore black trousers and a white shirt under his casual jacket.

"I've just come from work," he explained. "I told them I had an errand to do."

A1 for initiative, I thought.

"Please sit down," said Angela. "We won't keep you long."

"So, Fran, why do you want this job?" I said.

"Because the pay is good."

"And?" I prompted, having expected a more eloquent answer, as I'd seen lots of interviews on TV over the years.

He shrugged his narrow shoulders. "It's a nice place, or will be."

I glanced at my crib sheet. "And, er... what are your strong points?"

His rather dull brown eyes widened a tad. "I turn up on time and do my work well. I don't get ill."

I looked at my list of typical interview questions and decided to improvise.

"Does it bother you that the initial contract will only be for six months?"

He shrugged. "Not really. The contract I have now isn't worth a... isn't very good."

I smiled, having deduced that he'd been about to say mierda, or shit. "I see."

"And the pay is bad. Here the pay is good, so I want to work here." He glanced at his watch.

"Can you get references?"

"From my boss, but only if the job here is definite. Not from my last boss, as he did a runner."

He told me where he'd done a runner from and I knew of the man. He'd taken over a bar near the market, neglected to pay his suppliers and workers, and hopped it after four or five months. I also remembered Inma telling me how poorly most bar and restaurant staff were paid in the town, so Angela's offer of ten percent above average wages was bound to be a big increase.

"Do you speak any English?"

"Yes, but not very well. I can try to improve."

"Would you be able to start on May 1st?"

"Yes, or before. I'm a good worker. Ask anyone."

I asked him to wait outside for a moment.

"He's all right," I told Angela. "I've seen him work and he knows what he's doing."

"When he walked in I wondered why he wasn't wearing a tie, but it doesn't seem to matter now. He's a no-nonsense sort of lad, isn't he?"

"Yes. Shall we tell him we'll get in touch?"

"Ask him to come in, please."

Angela then told him in her slow but correct Spanish that she'd like him to start on the first of May.

He smiled for the first time. "Really? Full time?"

"Yes, you are our first employee and I hope you will be the best."

"Great, thank you. Oh, and references?"

"Not necessary, in your case," she said. "We will post the contract. The first days will be training and cleaning."

We all shook hands and he walked contentedly out, before jogging to his car and shooting off down the drive.

"He seems all right," I said.

"Yes."

"Should I have asked more questions?"

"Not really. Let's just trust our instincts. Look." She pulled her expensive watch around to the inside of her wrist. "If I pull it round again, that's like a thumbs up sign. That way we don't have to ask them to leave the room."

"But if you don't I might go on asking these questions until doomsday."

She laughed. "If I don't like them I'll start drumming my fingers on the table. Then just tell them that we'll get in touch. We can write them an email later."

I walked to the window and saw a plump woman in her forties step out of the passenger seat of a shiny Citroen C3. I invited her in and we got straight down to business. She also wanted the job –

of chambermaid – because the pay was good. She usually cleaned individual houses for cash, so the opportunity to work at least five hours straight was one not to be missed. When I mentioned the six-month contract she said that was fine, not having had any kind of contract since the time she'd worked in a school canteen. Her daughter had made the application, she explained, as she was useless on the computer. She seemed like a simple soul really, and her only problem was that she didn't drive.

"But I have a friend who does. If you give her a job too I can come with her."

Angela's hands remained motionless.

"Has she applied for the job?" I asked.

"No, but she's in the car now."

"Please ask her to come in," said Angela, and so it was that we secured two of the three chambermaids in twenty minutes.

When the women had gone, both chuffed to bits, I asked Angela if we weren't being a bit hasty.

"Do you think we are?"

"Not so far. I mean, all three of them see working here as being so much better than what they're doing now that I don't think they'll let us down."

"No, and if they do I've a feeling that there'll be plenty more willing people waiting in the wings. Is the job situation really so bad here?"

"I think so. Spain still hasn't recovered from the crash ten years ago, and I'm not sure things were so great for unqualified people before that either."

"Malcolm said we'd get a lot of people spouting a load of bullshit, but that doesn't seem to be the case at all."

"No, it's been straightforward so far."

The last interviewee was a pretty, bespectacled young lady who had applied for one of the receptionist-administrator roles.

She crept nervously into the room, sat shyly down, and on being asked why she wanted the job began to spout a load of bullshit.

"… so I feel that I have the right aptitudes and qualifications for the job due to my university studies and periods of work experience," she finally concluded after reeling off the most monotonous soliloquy since I auditioned unsuccessfully for the role of Hamlet in the sixth-form play.

'Chill out, babe,' I felt like saying, having slumped into the posture of Chandler's *Philip Marlowe, Private Eye*. 'You're a cute little broad, so shelve the speechifying and tell us what's really on your mind, honey,' I went on to myself, until Angela nudged me.

"Ah, yes, so… er, don't you think you're a little overqualified to be a receptionist, Sara?"

She gazed at me sadly. "No, most people who take the Tourism degree begin by working as a receptionist or something similar."

Angela perused her CV. "So, you studied in Valencia for three years, but you still haven't worked."

"No, I've done three placements, but I haven't done paid work yet. I think I get too nervous in interviews," she said with a nervous titter. "But I'm hard-working and I speak English and French, and a little Italian and German. I just need a chance."

Angela turned her watch and we signed her up for six months. She almost skipped across the gravel to her old car.

"Four out of four," Angela said.

"Yes, er… do you think we ought to employ everyone who comes?"

She laughed. "Of course not, but why not give them a chance if they seem willing? They did apply very quickly, apart from Elena, and if they don't work out we'll have no problem finding replacements."

"I agree. So, four down, about… fourteen to go. It still sounds like rather a lot of staff for a small hotel. How many bookings have you got so far?"

"Four."

"Ah."

"But there's still time."

"Yes, a month till the first course."

"I might lower the price a bit more, just to get bums on seats, and in beds. We'll need a good website too."

I failed to turn my cringe into a smile. "Yes."

"Ha, don't worry, Alan. It's being designed as we speak by a professional company, with my input. Even though I've been at home and on holiday, I've been taking care of everything, except the recruitment, which I thought I'd left a little late, but I'm not so sure about that now."

"So is everything else ordered?"

"Yes." She chuckled. "Test me."

I looked around for inspiration. "Curtains?"

"Yes, and blinds."

"Carpets?"

"No carpets, but plenty of rugs."

"Er, kitchen equipment?"

"In the hands of a Spanish supplier."

"All the furniture?"

"Ditto, and towels and bedding and decorations and everything else you can imagine."

I dug deep, determined to catch her out. "A phone system?"

"Ordered."

I pictured myself in a bedroom. "Kettles, hair-dryers, little fridges?"

"Yes, yes, yes."

"Tellies?"

"Only one, in here, and I trust it won't be used very often. The guests I'm hoping to attract won't be fond of the box, I hope."

"A fancy door-locking system?"

"No, just standard locks with nice big keys."

"All the little bottles and sachets that people pinch?"

"Yes, I suppose we'll have to have those. Come on, it's the weekend and I'm keeping you here. As Inma's free today I'm going to take you both out for a good lunch."

At 9.10am on Monday the recruitment agency informed Angela that they'd so far had well over a thousand applications for the jobs, so we were both ever so glad that they were selecting suitable candidates and forwarding their CVs.

"Just imagine if we'd done it ourselves, Alan," she said in the car.

"Yes, we'd have inboxes like... like telephone directories," I said, as my wit usually sharpens gradually throughout the day.

During the twenty-minute drive Angela's phone pinged constantly, each email being a single selected application.

"Waiter, waiter, receptionist, waitress, cook, chambermaid, waitress... oh, a male chambermaid, however you say that in English."

"Are you sure he isn't a waiter?" I said, as the term for chambermaid is *camarera de habitación*, or room waitress.

"No, he's a *camarero de habitación* all right. Still, we mustn't be sexist. Where's Orihuela?"

"Between Alicante and Murcia. Too far to travel every day, I'm afraid."

"Yes, and I want local people. Oh, well. Hmm, I'm not getting any applications for caretaker, maintenance man, gardener or chauffeur. I wonder why that is."

"I think some of those people won't be too hot on the computer."

"Hmm, I'm sure we'll miss some good workers by only advertising online."

I tapped my forehead. "But you already have a caretaker, haven't you?"

"Oh, that old man is just… well, let's say he's in charge of security or something. He wanted us to pay him in cash for keeping an eye on the place, so I'll go on giving him his two hundred a month." Her phone was still pinging away. "Waitress, receptionist, waiter… hmm, these people are on the ball, but–"

"Look!" I cried, unable to contain my excitement upon having one of my all too infrequent eureka moments.

"What? That's Arturo, isn't it?"

"Yes, he's our man."

"What for?"

"For maintenance man, gardener, chauffeur and whatever else you want him to be. Arturo's a true man for all seasons, unless you don't like the look of him."

"Of course I do. He's quite handsome and somehow… exotic. Very charming too, but doesn't he like building work?"

"He likes it well enough, but I have a feeling that he won't be sad to part company with Cristóbal. They tolerate each other, but Arturo's a free spirit and he's a rather bossy boss. I can ask him if he's interested if you like."

"All right, but later. Let's get ready for our first manager interview."

# 13

It's an uncanny coincidence that I should bring Gerardo into the picture at the beginning of Chapter *Thirteen*, and to this day I'm not sure if his arrival was lucky or unlucky for me. When the trim, slim man of about thirty-five walked into the room in his three-piece suit I didn't like the look of him at all. I didn't like his brown, sparkling but disturbingly deep-set eyes, or his fastidiously trimmed goatee beard and silly sideburns, or his limp handshake, or his charmingly insincere smile, or his slightly high-pitched voice and the carefully articulated words it produced, or his pointy shoes, or the fact that he scarcely looked at me once he knew that Angela was the owner. In short, I wasn't fond of the chap, but Angela was, so he got the job.

It turned out that he was a native of Almansa and had returned home from Preston because his mother had fallen ill. He had nursed her during the eighteen blank months on his CV, but couldn't bring himself to mention it therein, as her subsequent death still distressed him deeply. After that he'd decided to work locally for a while, until he regained the strength to resume his serious hotel career.

"I see. I'm sorry," I said, not sure whether to believe him or not.

"Oh, poor man, that's really awful," Angela said, after which she conducted the rest of the interview in English while I sat there like a spare part.

My suspicions may sound insensitive, but even if his story were true, the way he exploited his mother's illness and death in a job interview struck me as a piece of carefully calculated emotional blackmail which wouldn't have washed with many people, but appeared to convince Angela. Later when he expressed an unwillingness to request a reference from the big hotel in Preston, instead asking her to settle for ones from London and Almansa, my suspicions that things had gone awry for him in Lancashire increased.

Although Angela undoubtedly had a soft spot for Gerardo, she did ask him all the questions on her list, and it turned out that he ticked every box, down to his willingness to start soon.

"The hotel in Almansa is now running smoothly and they know that I wish to further my career, so I'm sure I'll be able to lower my workload there and begin to assist you almost immediately," he said with perfect grammar but a typically naff accent, as most Spaniards just can't seem to manage anything approaching an English one.

"I... Alan and I are recruiting now, but if you could assist with that, I'd be grateful," she said.

He graced me with a wolfish smile. "Of course. I have recruited many members of staff before and am aware of the qualities that are required. I would be more than happy to assist you in this task, from tomorrow, if you like."

*(I confess that at this exact point in my story I wasn't sure whether to ham it up in order to get some laughs out of Gerardo's manner and my reaction to it, or to avoid doing so lest I appear to be a bitter and twisted individual. I'm not one of those, I assure you, so I'll go on as planned.)*

...if you like," he said like Kenneth Williams of *Carry On* film fame.

*(But I won't overdo it.)*

…if you like," he said in a rather fawning way.

"Oh, that's wonderful, isn't it, Alan?"

"Yes. Yes, it is."

"Well, I'm delighted to offer you the job of manager, Gerardo."

"Pending references," I said.

"Yes, pending references, of course, but I'm sure they'll be fine."

"I assure you they will be," he said with a simper. "So have you already employed other staff?"

"Once we've taken up your refer–"

"Yes, four people. I'll tell you about them," she said, and she did, despite not having checked his references, which I believe she never got around to doing.

"They sound quite satisfactory, Angela. I'm sure we'll be able to assemble a great team and make this venture a super success," he said, gesticulating with his refined little hands that hadn't done a real day's work in their lives.

She fluttered her eyelashes and might have hugged him had the desk not been in the way. She'd never fluttered her eyelashes at me and I began to suspect that he was the type of man she secretly found attractive – physically feeble, sycophantic and slightly camp – rather than big, no-nonsense macho men like Malcolm and me. As they prattled on about how great and super it was going to be, I found myself wondering what Malcolm would make of Gerardo. He would detest the toadying little prig, of course, and lament his wife's unwise choice, but as Angela could do no wrong in his eyes, he'd probably try to be nice to him.

"When will Malcolm be coming?" I managed to ask during a lull.

They both seemed a bit surprised that I was still there.

"I'll go home in a few days, then come out with Malcolm as soon as he's able."

Gerardo smoothed his impeccable charcoal grey trousers and stood up. He patted his cute little quiff and beamed at his new employer.

"I'm afraid I must go now, as I have to work this afternoon, but I'll be here at nine tomorrow, if that's convenient for you, Angela."

She stood up. "Oh, Gerardo, you mustn't tire yourself by doing two jobs at once."

He tittered. "It isn't a problem, Angela. I'm used to hard work and I'm extremely keen on this new project."

"Isn't it a long way to drive from Almansa every day?" she asked.

"Only fifty minutes, and I'll find the time useful to run over the tasks of the day."

I stood up and was pleased to see a promising little bald patch on the back of his rather large head. On taking Angela's hand I thought he was going to curtsey, but he gave her a neat little bow instead. When he deigned to offer me his hand I enveloped it in my rough, powerful paw and pressed until I felt the metacarpals shatter into tiny fragments. Well, not quite, but I did give it a good hard squeeze, just to show him the type of guy he was dealing with.

"Now that you're on board, Gerardo, Alan will be able to concentrate on supervising the building work."

"Yes," I boomed, towering over the little shrimp of about five foot seven.

"That's good. I too will be around to ensure that all the equipment and fittings are installed to our satisfaction," he said.

I thought he might have overstepped the mark this time, as this was Angela's territory, but she just gushed a few more words of gratitude.

I don't wish to imply that Angela had lost her head over this Machiavellian little man, as she's pretty shrewd and must have sensed my antipathy towards him, because as we accompanied him out to his compact BMW she said the following.

"My greatest interest in the hotel will be the courses I've told you about."

"They sound wonderful," he crooned.

"Yes, and I believe Alan's going to assist me with them. Isn't that right, Alan?"

"Oh yes."

"So you'll be able to concentrate on the running of the hotel. Well, I look forward to seeing you tomorrow."

"Yes, bye for now, Angela."

"Hasta mañana, Gerardo," I said.

"Yes, see you tomorrow," the little blighter said in English, thus commencing one of the greatest battles for linguistic hegemony in the history of mankind, as I'd be damned if I was going to speak English to him when Angela wasn't present.

When he'd driven away Angela reminded me that I was going to have a word with Arturo.

"Ah, yes, I'll go and find him."

She smiled. "I'll take a stroll on the new lawns. I hope the joins will… join up before the first guests arrive."

I found Arturo upstairs, tiling a bathroom wall alone.

"Al-an! How's it going?"

OK. Listen, I was going to suggest that you work at the hotel, doing maintenance, gardening, driving and whatnot, but Angela's just taken on a manager who I don't think you'll like, so maybe it isn't a good idea after all," I babbled.

"Hey, calm down, man. You're all stressed." He patted my arm with his cleaner left hand.

"Yes, well, what do I tell her? Are you interested?"

"Tell her I might be, if the wages are good. I reckon Cristóbal will lay me off after this job anyway, unless something big comes up, but there's no need to tell her that. I'll check out this new manager guy, and we'll see what he thinks of me. All right?"

"Yes."

"Take it easy, Alan."

"Yes, I will."


I suggested at the beginning of this fateful chapter that I wasn't sure if the appearance of Gerardo was a good thing for me or not, and I was soon able to see the silver lining around this bothersome cloud, so when we drove back to the house my feeling of annoyance was tempered by a growing sense of relief. Gerardo, despite his numerous flaws (in my eyes), appeared to have the expertise to run a little hotel like Angela's with his eyes closed, so my worries on that score were over. From then on, anything that went wrong would be their fault, not mine, so when Angela, after leaving me to mull things over for a while, said that she suspected I didn't think as highly of Gerardo as she did, I was able to reply with equanimity.

"Oh, I admit that he's not really my cup of tea, but I think he'll do a good job."

"Yes, I think so too. I really think I should stay at the hotel in town from tonight. I've imposed myself on you and Inma for quite long enough."

Sensing a test, I protested. "Nonsense, you'll stay with us until you go back. I'll drive you to the hotel every day and I'll help out with the building as I was about to do when you arrived."

"Make sure Cristóbal pays you then. Malcolm knows that he's making a packet out of the work, you know."

"Does he?"

"Yes, but he can't be bothered to haggle over a few thousand. He's much softer now than he used to be, and he's pleased that the total cost of the completed hotel will be less than he budgeted for. So, as I said, I hope you'll help me with the courses when they start."

"Yes, I'd like that."

"And we'll leave the running of the hotel to Gerardo."

"Yes."

"And I'll make it clear that the courses aren't his remit, but yours and mine."

"Yes."

She chuckled. "I hope I've put your mind at rest."

Yes, I… yes."

"Gerardo's arrival will be all for the best, you'll see."

"Yes, I hope so."

As Inma arrived home quite late from the bar, Angela cooked a delicious stew for dinner and went off to her room at her usual early hour. When I happened to pass by her door in order to check the damp patch in the end room, I heard her speaking softly. Feeling a sudden cramp in my left calf, I was forced to remain immobile for a few moments and I soon deduced that she was talking to her husband, extolling the virtues of the Angel of Almansa. My damn cramp just wouldn't go away.

"Alan doesn't like him much and you probably won't either, but I know his sort from meeting employees of yours and he's perfect for the job."

(Pause while M spoke.)

"No, I mean that he's one of those self-serving types who'll work like hell to get the place up and running, then probably move on to somewhere else. He knows his stuff and I'm going to pick his brains, so by the time he leaves I'll be more on the ball. I feel pretty clueless now and Alan's even worse than me, so we need this chap to get things going."

(Long pause while M spoke.)

"Yes, I know he seems to have come down in the world. From Madrid to London and then to Preston, of all places, doesn't make much sense, and I think he must have messed up there and got sacked or something. I could call the hotel where he worked, but I probably won't bother. So that's why he needs this job, to get his career back on track, as that place in Almansa sounds like an awful hole from the reviews I've read. I think you'll admire him in some ways, as he's a wonderful liar, every bit as good as some of your salesmen." She chuckled. "Anyway, if he's no good you'll know and you can give him his marching orders when we come back..."

By this time I really was in danger of getting cramp, so motionlessly had I stood, so I crept away and Inma and I soon went to bed. As she was tired I just gave her a brief summary of the day's events.

She yawned, unfazed by my dramatic finale. "It's better this way, I think. I mean, you don't really like responsibility, do you?"

"Well, not much, apart from my responsibilities to you, dear."

I kissed her and she was soon sound asleep.

# 14

The next morning I sprang out of bed and pulled on my overalls, my brain having decided during my slumbers how to approach the next few days. As soon as Angela appeared I served our breakfast items of orange juice, cereals, toast and coffee in rapid succession and by half past eight we were motoring down the lane to town.

"My, you seem keen today, Alan," she said with a chuckle.

"Ah, because I love working with my hands. I can't wait to get stuck in with the lads," I enthused.

"Make sure Cristóbal pays you properly."

"Yes, I'll ask him to pay me by the hour. That way we can come and go when we please."

Cristóbal immediately agreed with my suggestion and said that I could mix and/or carry for however long I wanted, in return for which he'd pay me twelve euros an hour, cash in hand. The fact that Angela was standing with her arms folded some five yards away may have had some bearing on his acquiescence, but by the time Gerardo arrived, in a two-piece suit today, I was upstairs with Arturo, waiting for him to finish his fag.

I beckoned him to the window. "Arturo, he's here now. Look how he walks, like a constipated cat."

"Hmm, but the guy has style."

"Has he?"

"Oh, yes, and I love the shoes. Just watch how I make friends with him."

"He might not like gypsies, or half gypsies."

"Haven't I got on fine with all these ignorant workmen?"

"Yes, you have, even Cristóbal. Come on, let's finish this wall."

I remained upstairs all morning, laying a few vertical tiles like a past master, and when Angela came to find me I was still hard at it.

"We've just interviewed three more people, Alan."

"Ah," I said, making sure that the superbly centred spirit level bubble was within her line of vision, though I don't think she noticed.

"Gerardo didn't like one of them. I'd have taken him on, but I'll let him decide, as the staff are his responsibility."

"Uh-huh," I murmured absently as I reached for another tile.

She sniggered softly, before asking Arturo how things were going.

"Fine, Señora. Alan and I are making good progress here."

She asked him if he'd considered my proposal of the previous day.

"I'm certainly interested, in principle, if the hours are enough and I fit in with the new… team," he said slowly. "I like it here in the country and I enjoy doing different tasks, so yes, I'm interested."

"Can you start on the first of May?"

"Yes, Señora, if we agree on the wages."

"Is the same as what you're earning now all right?"

"Yes. And the hours?"

"Is forty all right?"

"Perfect," he said with his most charming smile – sincerely charming, not like Gerardo's – before whipping off his gloves and tossing them into the sink. "May I kiss your hand to seal our deal, Señora?"

She laughed. "No, you may not, and please call me Angela."

"All right, Angela."

"Speak to Gerardo about the paperwork."

"Is he the dapper little man who looks so important?" he asked, the cheeky so-and-so.

"Ha, yes, that's him. Alan and I are going now, but he'll be here until about four. Have a word with him later."

"I will, thank you."

"Er, won't Gerardo want to... er, interview him or something?" I murmured in English.

"I've told him that Arturo is my appointment," she said in Spanish. "We three will be independent of Gerardo. Do you both understand that?"

We said we did.

In the car she was prodding her phone, so I asked her if she was looking at more job applications.

"No, at flights. Could you take me to the airport later, please?"

"Yes, but so soon?"

"So soon after employing Gerardo, you mean? Yes, I'll go now and fly back with Malcolm in a week or so."

"Do you trust Gerardo with everything?"

"Yes, I think so, but please keep an eye on him, and ask Arturo to do so too."

"I must say I think it was brilliant of you to take on Arturo in that way."

"I can be shrewd sometimes, Alan."

"Yes."

She chuckled. "Cristóbal doesn't think much of Gerardo, unsurprisingly."

"Doesn't he? I've hardly seen either of them this morning."

"Yes, I've noticed your policy of splendid isolation. I asked Cristóbal to keep an eye on… things too, so I'll hopefully have three pairs of eyes I can count on, then two after we open."

I was almost looking forward to seeing Gerardo the following day and subtly hinting at my special powers.

"Divide and rule," I said spontaneously.

"Yes, Malcolm's taught me all about that. He's looking forward to coming out."

"I'll drive the Hymer over one day soon."

"Thank you. Please park it opposite the front door, pointing towards it."

"I will."

"Malcolm likes to keep an eye on things, you see."

"Yes."

"From the driving seat."

"Definitely. I'm looking forward to seeing him."

"You know, I think you really are this time, Alan."

I laughed and reminded myself never, ever to underestimate people again.


That Saturday I cycled to Cathy and Bernie's, from where he drove the Hymer to the hotel while I followed in Letizia. After guiding him into position, about fifteen yards from the front door, I locked up the Hymer and we went inside.

"Is everything all right, Gerardo?" I asked him in Spanish after entering the little room that was to become his office.

"Yes, just fine," he replied in English. "I have four people to interview this morning for the position of chef. I also have appointments with two food suppliers later, so I hope to introduce the successful candidate to them."

"That's good. Angela will be pleased that everything is slowly coming together," I said in Spanish.

"Not so slowly," he replied in English with a loathsome leer. (In fact you can take it as read that Gerardo and I will converse in this absurd bilingual way when we're alone together, unless I indicate otherwise.)

Although Bernie was hovering in the doorway, I had no intention of introducing him. For all Gerardo knew, he might be another of Angela's appointments.

"Malcolm and Angela will be arriving on Wednesday," I said.

"I know."

I allowed my lips to twitch. "Malcolm is looking forward to meeting you."

"I know, and I too am looking forward to meeting him."

I glanced at the papers on his desk. "Yes, see you later." I turned to Bernie. "Come on, I'll show you round," I said, still in Spanish.

"What's with the language game, Alan?" he said as I led him into the future dining room.

"Not a game, but a battle. I will *not* speak English to Spaniards in Spain, unless there's a good reason for it. It's a matter of principle, especially with a prick like him."

"What's up with him? He seems all right."

"Does he?"

"Yes, I mean, he's a bit poncy, but you're normally more tolerant about folk."

"Hmm, maybe I have taken a slightly irrational dislike to him, but it's a gut feeling I've got and I can't help it. I'll show you the bedrooms."

"Ha, the cunning little git," Bernie said when I'd told him how Gerardo had used his mother's death to elicit sympathy in the interview.

"I think it was out of order, especially if it's not true."

"Well, if it's not true I suppose it is a bit much, but that's the way of the world, Alan. If you need a job, you do whatever it takes to get it."

"It's not my way."

"No, but then you were never much of a one for jobs, were you?"

I stiffened. "I've had jobs."

"Yes, but mostly crap ones that were easy to get. If you *really* want to get a certain job, you do whatever it takes."

"Yes, you said."

"It's dog eat dog in the world of work, Alan, and you have to remember that. Anyway, Angela's already got him sussed, so it doesn't matter."

"No, I guess not. What do you think of the place?"

"It's going to be pretty smart. Come on, let's get back and I'll show you my land."

After whirring along the back roads for half an hour, enjoying the sunny morning with the roof rolled back, we arrived at the field, where Spartacus stood poised with his old but rust-free plough attached.

"Wow, you've transformed it, Bern," I said as I surveyed the long stretch of dry, thoroughly ploughed earth.

He adjusted his not yet battered straw hat. "Yes, I've been over it a few times."

"How many?"

"Oh, about half a dozen. Each time you break up the earth a little more, you see."

I chuckled. "You're not going to turn into another Jesús, are you?"

"Course not, though ploughing can be a bit addictive. Despite the noise, it's quite soothing. I tell Cathy it's my way of meditating, but she just laughs."

"Is she at home?" I said, looking forward to seeing my sis.

"No, she's meditating and doing yoga. She gone on a retreat to the Sierra Espuña," he said, referring to a mountain to the south-west of Murcia.

"Right. She must be getting keen on her yoga then."

"Yes, and the folk she meets there. They're mostly women, locals and foreigners, and she loves going. She still sees her oldies too, of course."

"So I suppose she's feeling more satisfied at last."

"Yes." He looked up and sighed. "And I'll be satisfied when my field gets a good dousing and I can get the olive trees planted. It's a waiting game at the moment."

I pictured the field dotted with little olive trees, but couldn't imagine what he'd do there except plough, as they wouldn't need pruning for a long time. I hoped he wasn't getting bored and spending too much time in the bar.

"Come on, I'll show you the allotment."

After harvesting mediocre crops of potatoes, onions and garlic, a few bags of which he'd taken to the bar, Bernie had planted some more. The rest of the allotment lay fallow and composted, awaiting the transplantation of the dozen or so seed trays which he brought out into the sun each day, before covering them on the porch at night, or even taking them inside when night-time temperatures had fallen too low. Much of this he'd done since we returned from our trip.

"The really cold nights have been over for a while now, and it'll soon be time to transplant the tomatoes, spinach, aubergines and whatnot. I'm trying some coriander and a few other things too, but I shan't bother with radishes again, as no-one seems to like them."

"I'm impressed, Bernie."

He shrugged and tipped back his hat. "I'm just doing what most country folk do around here."

I pictured the blackening almond trees on our abandoned strips of land and felt ashamed. There I was, involving myself in a luxury hotel which well-heeled foreigners would visit to mess about with paintbrushes, pens or musical instruments, while my own backyard was a complete disgrace. Typical guiri, the neighbours must think – apart from Álvaro, who lived a life of the mind – though I consoled myself with the thought that they too might own abandoned land, as there were many more fields like mine in the upper reaches of the valley.

I sighed. "I really should do something with our land."

"I can't drive Spartacus over there, I'm afraid. You could get someone to rip out the trees and plough it, but then you'd have to get them to plough it regularly, so you might as well just leave it for now. It's not coming to any harm, after all. I'll tell you what you could do, though."

"What?"

"Has the annex got an outside tap?"

"Yes, and Arturo put a new one on."

"Well, you could dig over the nearest bit of land, then water it with a long hose and dig it over again. Then I'll give you a few of these pots to plant and you could try some seeds too."

"Yes, I could," I said without much enthusiasm.

He slapped me on the back. "Ha, you'll soon finish grafting at the hotel, then you can dig it over in May. Don't do too much and keep it simple, then at least you'll have made a start. It's nature who does most of the work anyway, and she won't be slow like last autumn. Now things'll really grow." He rubbed his hands together and grinned. "I can't wait to see everything starting to shoot up."

Although this was by no means the first pep talk Bernie had given me over the years, it was a surprisingly successful one, as no sooner had I cycled home than I changed my shoes and set about the nearest bit of field with the mattock he'd lent me. As it was rock hard I decided on a plot of about five square yards, doing the corners first in order to force myself to finish it. While I was thwacking away I saw a hunched figure out of the corner of my eye. This turned out to be Zefe, trying to sneak into the annex without me seeing him.

"Hey, you old devil, I thought Álvaro was supposed to be taking you home yesterday," I cried, raising my mattock in a menacing manner.

He cowered comically. "Oh, Alan, he was going to, but... his car broke down."

"Ha, I bet I could go there now and start it straight away."

"Yes, you could, because he fixed it."

"What was up with it?"

"Er, a dirty carburettor."

Although I couldn't imagine Álvaro dismantling a pen, let alone a carburettor, I let it pass, because one must respect one's elders, even rogues like Zefe. As I still felt a bit guilty about banishing him during Natalia's fictitious visit, I said he might as well stay and go home the following Thursday.

"Without fail," I added sternly.

"Thank you, Alan. Now that the sun is getting warmer, my old joints are becoming less stiff. Look." He walked around in a circle with his stick over his shoulder. "Here I feel younger every day, and I can even walk up onto your marvellous new patio, but in my damp flat my rheumatism plays up."

"Your flat isn't the least bit damp, but I see what you mean."

I recalled watching the film of Alan Bennett's book, *The Lady in the Van*, shortly before coming to Spain, and later discovering that the main reason the lady had camped on his drive for so many years was because she'd obtained squatter's rights. Did squatter's rights exist in Spain and might Zefe get them if he stayed for too long? I wondered.

"Do you always wear cycling clothes when you work on the land, Alan?"

"Not always," I said, before explaining what I intended to do.

"That's wonderful, Alan."

"Yes, er... why?"

"Because in summer when one wishes to make a salad, one will be able to step outside and pick the ingredients."

"Yes, one will, unless one never eats salads, like you."

"Hmm, will you plant onions?"

I laughed. "Yes, if you like."

When I'd changed into more appropriate clothing and eaten some lunch, I returned to my plot and saw that Zefe had gone down to Álvaro's again. I wondered if it would ever occur to the retired teacher to take Zefe in as a lodger. That would avoid a lot of toing and froing and he might be rewarded for his altruism by inheriting his estate, and what riches might Zefe have amassed during his adventurous life? A goldmine in Brazil? A croft in Iceland? Probably just the flat and a bit of money in the bank, I mused as I hacked away at the earth.

# 15

On Monday and Tuesday I mostly stayed out of Gerardo's way, only emerging from the bedroom I was putting the finishing touches to with Arturo to spy on him periodically. My spying consisted of walking downstairs and around the ground floor for no reason whatsoever, pausing whenever I saw him and observing him pointedly for a few seconds, before moving on. I didn't do this merely to annoy him, but because Angela had asked me to keep an eye on things, so when he asked me if I was looking for someone I smiled enigmatically and slowly shook my head. He then shook his head, presumably in exasperation, before clumping stiffly back into his office. On telling Arturo that I had the little twerp rattled, he said I was being childish.

"It's his fault. If he spoke to me in Spanish I might answer him," I said with childish petulance. "And why does he have to dress up every day as if he were going to a wedding?"

Arturo laid his trowel on the tray and shook *his* head. "Alan, for a man of fifty you're remarkably immature in some ways."

"Fifty-one," I muttered, having celebrated my birthday quietly with Inma the previous month.

"The poor guy's just trying to assert himself. He dresses well because new recruits are arriving every day and he must show them he's the boss. He wishes to speak to you in English so that people see that he can. All this is perfectly normal in his position. The world of work is like that. At least give the man a chance, Alan."

"Ha, he'll see who the real boss is tomorrow when Malcolm arrives," I said with a cackle, but as the day wore on I reflected on Arturo's wise words and realised that I ought to shelve my infantile side and give him the benefit of the doubt for the time being, though I still wouldn't answer him in English if we were alone, oh no, not that.

On arriving home Inma told me she had some good news and some bad news.

"Tell me the good news first."

"Bernie sold my car, for €850."

"That's a great price for the old thing. And the bad news?"

"I spoke to Natalia on the phone earlier."

"Is she coming? That's not bad news at all, dear, as we're getting on fine."

"I haven't finished."

"Oh, go on."

"She wants to know if you've arranged her summer job at the hotel yet."

"Ah, yes, well, that's a bit tricky just now, what with this new idi..." I remembered my resolution just in time. "...manager. Tell her I'm doing my best to arrange it."

"She needs to make plans, she says."

I reviewed my current standing at the hotel and remembered that the courses were going to be my thing.

"Tell her I'll arrange it after the first course, assuming it's a success."

"All right, I'll tell her that you've already fallen out with the manager and that the courses are her only hope."

I told her about my new, mature attitude towards Gerardo.

"Well, I hope you stick to it. In the world of work one must try to behave professionally."

"Ah, the world of work has been a closed book to me."

"Well try to open it, at least for a while."

The next time I saw Gerardo I was with Malcolm and Angela, so I was able to speak to him in English without offending my linguistic sensibilities. When they arrived in a posh hire car I happened to be outside, so I greeted them warmly and headed towards the door, but the big man called me back.

"I want to see my Hymer first. Have you got the keys?"

I trotted over to my Clio to fetch them. "We cleaned it thoroughly," I said.

He smiled. "I don't doubt it, but I'm dying to see her again."

"He's been looking forward to this all morning," Angela said as he bounded around in the van, seeming truly delighted to be there.

"There's something about motorhomes that I love. Shame I was so busy for so long. We'll put her round the side though, as I don't want to see everyone coming and going all the time."

"We thought you might," she said.

"No, the hotel's your thing, love. Do you play golf, Alan?"

"Er, I've played pitch and putt a few times," I mumbled.

He grimaced. "Still, until I find someone decent to play with you'll have to do."

I began to gulp, but my Adam's apple stayed put. "You know, I think I'd enjoy that."

Angela laughed. "He takes it terribly seriously though. He's ever so competitive."

"No, not with a rookie. Come on, I suppose I'd better meet the man of the moment."

"Gerardo seems to be doing a very good job," I said.

Angela smirked. "Have you been drinking, Alan?"

I chuckled. "No, just being positive. I've realised that in the world of work you have to put your personal feelings aside."

"I never did," said M.

"You didn't need to," said A.

"And he really has been working hard," said I, before telling them about his recruitments and other sundry matters that seemed to interest Malcolm little or not at all.

"He's determined not to get involved if he sees that things are going well," Angela said.

Malcolm had stopped and was looking at my feet. "What size do you take?"

"Usually tens."

"My spare golf shoes'll be no good then, as they're thirteens. Right, lead me to him."

Gerardo looked especially small and weedy beside Malcolm, but his smart attire did lend him an air of authority; that and the fact that he soon began to reel off a list of his accomplishments, which included securing almost all of the staff, liaising with the assessors, ordering everything that Angela had overlooked, and ensuring that Cristóbal stuck to his schedule. Malcolm nodded, grunted and glanced out of the window at the acre or so of fallow farmland behind the hotel.

"What are you planning to do with that, love?"

"Nothing yet, just keep it tidy. Eugenio will plough it before we open," she said, referring to the elderly caretaker cum security man.

"Hmm, a great big lawn would look nicer," he said, moving both his hands to the right as if about to make a swing.

Angela spotted this and stroked his arm. "No, dear, we're not having any golf facilities here."

"I could knock a ball around a lawn," he muttered. "So, Gerardo," he boomed. "You seem to have everything under control, so we'll leave you to it for now."

"Yes, Malcolm."

Malcolm turned to leave.

"I'll stay with Gerardo for a while," said Angela.

"OK, love. Come on, Alan."

As we were making our way out, Cristóbal appeared at the top of the stairs.

"Everything all right, Chris?" Malcolm bellowed.

"Yes, yes."

"Good, good," he said, before stomping outside with me in his wake. "Can't be bothered talking to him right now." He looked me up and down, as if for the first time. "Why are you dressed like a navvy?"

"Because I'm working here, for Cristóbal, with Arturo."

"Not today, lad, because *we* have work to do."

It transpired that our work consisted of finding the best golf course in the area, so after driving me home to change – 'Nice cave house you've got here, Alan. Hurry up.' – we headed north and then west to the town of Villena where the first course on his list was situated, next to a big tennis academy. Fortunately we'd had time for a bite to eat in the restaurant before Malcolm discovered the true nature of the golf course.

"Bah, it's just a glorified pitch and bloody putt course," he growled, tossing the revelatory leaflet onto the table.

I folded it and put it in my pocket. "It might be a good place to practise though, and it's only twenty-odd miles from the hotel," I said, as the par-three holes appealed to me. I hadn't been too bad at pitch and putt, you see, but had never wielded a wood in my life.

"Hmm, we'll see. Right, we're off down the motorway towards Alicante now to see another one."

The *Font del Llop Golf Resort*, just past the small town of Monforte del Cid, proved to be more to Malcolm's liking, and as we wandered along the edge of its proper eighteen-hole course he expressed his approval of the rolling fairways and smooth greens.

"This is more like it. Looks tricky but not too tricky."

"It's got nice ponds and lovely views."

"Hmm, let's go and see what the crack is," he said, before leading the way – Malcolm always led the way – into reception.

It turned out that one could just turn up, pay and play a round.

"This'll do for a start then," he said after leading the way back to the car.

"I wonder where they find the water to water it. They must consume a lot and the reservoirs are ever so low right now," I said, my conscience pricking me even before I'd pushed in a tee.

He looked at me and wrinkled his stubby nose. "Who cares? It's green, which is the main thing, and I hope it stays green all summer. We'd better get you kitted out before we play. Don't want you showing me up."

"What kit?"

"Proper jacket, trousers, shoes, gloves. You can use my clubs at first, before you buy your own."

I gulped. "I'm… I'm not *that* keen on golf really," I stuttered.

I expected him to scowl, but he grinned. "How do you know?"

"Well, it's just something I've never really taken to. Pitch and putt was enough for me, now and then, when someone suggested it."

"I haven't met a man yet who didn't take to golf."

"No?"

"No, apart from weaklings who can't walk or hit a ball or stand a bit of rain. You're not one of them, are you, Alan?"

"No, I'm not one of them. I don't mind having a go." I glanced across the road and made a fortuitous sighting. "Look, those two blokes have normal clothes on, and trainers."

"Hmm, I was going to drive you to Alicante and buy you the whole caboodle, but if you think you might get cold feet we won't bother yet. It's not like I want to force you to play, after all."

Emboldened by this rare moment of mildness, I expressed my desire to have a go on the Villena pitch and putt course first.

"Hmm."

"I might make a fool of myself on a proper course, you see."

"Hmm, you might. We'll go back to that mickey mouse course tomorrow then."

"Ah, yes, I'd love to, but I'm working for Cristóbal, remember? We could play on Saturday."

He looked at me in an almost, but not quite, pleading way. "I'm *itching* to play, Alan."

"I suppose I could have another afternoon off."

"Ach, stuff Cristóbal. He can soon find someone else."

"He does pay me though."

He clapped his hand on my shoulder and left it there, exerting considerable downward pressure. "Alan."

"Yes?"

"Don't be a penny pincher."

"No."

"Think in the longer term."

"Yes."

"Sooner or later I'll be having a house built."

"Yes."

"Assuming we like it here."

"Yes."

"And that depends on both Angela and me keeping ourselves busy, doing what we like doing."

"Ye... I see."

"You'll be contracting the builder for that house and you'll be getting your commission."

"Will I?"

"Yes, so you've no need to be grubbing around for a few pesetas or whatever they call money here."

"Right, I won't then."

"Think *big*, Alan," he said, finally removing his hand.

"Yes, I will."

He tapped his head. "In the world of work it pays to keep well in with the people who count."

"Yes, I suppose it does."

On the drive back up the motorway he looked at the clock and clicked his tongue. "No time for a round this aft. I'll pick you up at eight tomorrow."

"So early? I mean, I'll be up, but..."

"You don't think we're only going to play one round on that joke of a course, do you?"

"No, Malcolm."


You'll have noticed that I often end chapters by feeding back to Inma, and this one will be no exception.

She shook her head and laughed. "Oh, what a difference a day makes."

I cradled my head in my hands and rubbed my temples. "It's all a bit disturbing."

"Why?"

"Because I feel like I'm being manipulated. I'm putty in his great big hands."

"Go with the flow," she said in English.

"If I go with the flow I'll end up playing golf every day," I whined, also in English, my sweetheart being an exception to my otherwise strict language rule.

"Lucky you. At this time of year it will be very nice to be outside, hitting a little ball from time to time, or don't you like to be with Malcolm?"

"Oh, I like him well enough. Anyway, tomorrow when he sees how badly I play, he'll soon start looking elsewhere for a partner."

# 16

"Ooh, beginner's luck," I said after pitching my very first ball onto the edge of the green. It was a cool, sunny morning and we were the first people on the course, at nine o'clock on the dot. Malcolm had paid our fee – much cheaper than the real golf course we'd visited – and was visibly excited to be playing his first round for over a week, having been tied up by business matters back home. So excited, in fact, that he overhit his first shot, sending the ball over the green and under a tree.

"Used to whacking it when I tee off," he said with a shrug.

He walked fast for a big man and I saw that he was fitter than he looked. As soon as I'd putted my ball to within about three yards of the hole, he skilfully chipped his from under the tree and right over the green.

"I have a tendency to overhit, my coach says," he said cheerfully.

"Yes."

"He thinks it may be a psychological trait."

"Could be, as you always were a big hitter in business," I quipped.

He paused on his way across the green. "Still am, but please don't say stuff like that, as it reminds me of all the toadies I've played with over the years. Ha, I could go round in over a hundred and they'd still be praising my shots, the silly buggers. Right, get yours in... oh, bad luck."

He made an excellent putt, so we both scored four.

"Matchplay or stroke play, which do you prefer?" he asked.

"Er, what's the difference?"

He cringed. "Do you not watch golf on telly?"

"Not much. I remember Nick Faldo winning the British Open once."

"He won it three times, many moons ago. When did you last play?"

"Oh, about five years ago, I think."

He grinned. "Better make it matchplay then. We score each hole instead of adding up the shots."

"OK. Why is that better for me though?"

"You'll see."

On the second he overhit again, while I fluked a really good shot and got down in three, to his four.

"One up to you, Alan."

On the third I sliced my first shot, but recovered with the second and we both scored four. (Don't worry, I shan't be going on like this for long.)

On the fourth he got into the swing of things – ha, ha – and scored three, while I needed seven shots due to the intervention of a bunker.

"Put it behind you, Alan. That's the beauty of matchplay, you see."

"Yes."

And he was right, because apart from a bit of luck on the sixth and the ninth, where we drew, I made a real hash of the other holes.

"I enjoyed that," I said hopefully.

"The beauty of this silly little course, Alan, is that it's designed so you can play the same holes again, but from different tees."

"Oh, that's nice."

"So we can carry on and complete the eighteen without repeating ourselves. Quite clever really."

"Yes."

"Your shot."

Then my game really went to pieces, but Malcolm was kind enough to explain why on the seventeenth, where I'd landed in the pond before starting again and finding the bunker.

"When you don't play for a long time, you tend to start off all right. It's as if your brain's remembering how it's done and your body obeys, at first, but as you carry on you usually lose it and your game goes to pieces," he said patiently while I hacked away at the stupid bloody ball.

"Yes," I seethed.

"Try to relax."

I was no longer counting the shots and although the eighteenth was a bit better I was glad when it was over.

"Not bad for a first try," he said as we walked back to the clubhouse.

"It was bloody annoying when it all went wrong."

"Good thing we played matchplay, eh?"

"Yes."

"For me too, as I was none too hot myself. We'll get a bite to eat now."

"Yes."

"Then go round again."

I almost dropped the bag of seven or eight clubs that he'd allowed me to carry. "Again?"

He shrugged. "You can just stroll round and keep me company, if you like, but I think you'll find that you'll want to have another go in an hour or so."

"I doubt it, but I don't mind walking round."

In the event he was right, because when he slipped his tee into the mat my hands began to twitch.

He grinned and plucked another from his shirt pocket.

"I'd better go and pay for my round then," I said.

"Already paid. This time, if I were you, I wouldn't even count the shots. Just chat to me and don't worry about the game. You'll play better that way."

He was right again, as although I usually needed about five shots to get the ball down, I wasn't nearly as awful as I'd been before our break. Malcolm quizzed me about my life in Spain, something he'd never done before, but when I asked him about his life he became rather reticent.

"Oh, Alan," he finally said on the ninth, or twenty-seventh. "My life's just been work, work, work for the last thirty years. When I first expanded I thought things would get easier, being able to delegate, you know, but it just got more and more complicated."

"And you still haven't retired," I observed.

"Not properly, but I will. If we like it in Spain I'll get out of the food business once and for all."

"Do you think the hotel will do well?"

"Not really."

"No?"

He sighed, before hitting a lovely chip. "This is what I think will happen, Alan. Those courses will do all right, as long as the teachers or whatever you call them are decent, but the rest of the time there'll just be a few stray tourists who've stumbled across the place."

I thumped my ball through the grass in the right direction. "But they're going to advertise on those hotel websites."

"So what? Look, it's not on any major routes, there are no especially interesting places nearby, and though the countryside's all right, it's nothing to write home about, is it?"

"I guess not," I said, whacking my ball on the move. "Have you shared these thoughts with Angela?"

"I've told her not to get her hopes up too much. She only really wants arty-farty folk there anyway, so I can see the day when the place'll be open mainly for the courses and there'll be a lot less staff. It's bloody ridiculous the number of folk they've persuaded her to take on, but who cares? We'll keep the best and let the others go, including that sly little sod who's setting it all up for her."

"Then you'll have more time to go off in the Hymer."

"Exactly." He grasped the flag. "You help her to make those courses a big hit and the rest will take care of itself."

"Yes."

He pulled out the flag and performed a short, one-handed putt. "Get yours down and we'll be off."

I was delighted to sink a six-footer.

"Unless you want to go round again," he said, before cackling, slapping me on the back and steering me off the course.

"I think Malcolm's probably right about the hotel," said Inma after listening patiently to a blow by blow account of our game. "Although I hope he's wrong, as it will be a good thing for the area."

"He does have a habit of being right though. I guess it's his instinct that's made him successful in business. Anyway, he's given me a day off golf tomorrow. He says I'll play less badly if I have a rest, so he's going back to Villena and taking me to the proper course on Saturday, as I told him you were working. He's actually more considerate than he appears at first sight."

"You obviously like playing golf though, as you've told me so much about your game that I almost felt like I was there." She chuckled. "I hope you don't become obsessed by it like some men do."

I shook my head and tutted. "No chance of that. I admit that it's been fun to have a go again, and I wouldn't mind playing now and then, but it's not for me. I don't approve of all the water they use for a start. No, I'll humour Malcolm for now and just hope that he meets some people to play with soon." I narrowed my eyes and tapped my nose. "Anyway, in the world of work it pays to keep well in with the people who count, you know."

"Like Malcolm said."

"Yes, like Malcolm said."

The next day I worked at the hotel and on Saturday we played golf on the course near Monforte for the first time. We got there early to avoid the crowds, but it was busy anyway, which did nothing to improve my game, as when a man handles a wood for the first time he doesn't really want to have three impatient young blokes from the south of England standing nearby, tutting and sighing as he bungles shot after shot, Malcolm having decided that he ought to get the hang of it before commencing the game proper.

"You go to a driving range to do that," one of them finally muttered, upon which Malcolm bade them step up and go ahead of us, before standing two yards behind them, tutting, sighing, groaning and murmuring that they weren't much bloody good either, though I think his looming presence was affecting their swings somewhat.

"Right, let's try again," he said when they'd hurried away to find their widely dispersed balls.

It isn't easy to hit a golf ball straight with a wood, and despite Malcolm's sound advice I soon found myself faced with the choice of either whacking the thing and hoping for the best or playing a more conservative stroke but only making it about half way down the fairway, if that. He urged me to settle for this option, and by giving me a one-shot handicap we managed to have a fairly competitive game – he won by two holes – as he was happy to admit that he wasn't much of a player either.

"Eighty-four is my best ever score," he told me on the par-five fifteenth. "That was on a perfect day on an easy course and I played a blinder. I was walking on air for a week. I even picked up the phone when my salesmen called, just to tell them about it. A golfer lives for days like that, but they don't come around very often."

I gave the ball a good whack and sent it curling into the rough.

He sighed. "That pillock was right. You need to spend some time on a driving range, with a coach."

As he then hit a fine drive, I decided it was time to lay my golfing cards on the table.

"The odd game of pitch and putt is enough for me, Malcolm. I realise what it'd take to make me a half-decent player and I'm not really up for it. It's too expensive for one thing and it'd take up too much time to become any good. There are other things I prefer to do than play golf."

"Like what?" he said mildly.

"Oh, work on the land for one thing, and… well, other things, plus my work at the hotel, of course."

We found my ball and I managed to get it back on track with a six-iron.

"Good shot, Alan. You have a bit of ability, you know, but if you won't put the time in you'll never be any good. Still, I don't mind coming here on my own. There are plenty of foreigners and I'll soon meet someone to play with."

"Yes, there are quite a lot of them."

After a marvellous third shot on the eighteenth which left my ball within spitting distance of the hole, I reiterated that I wouldn't mind playing pitch and putt at Villena once in a while.

"Maybe once a week," I said, before sinking my putt. "Or twice."

"Ha, today your drive has let you down, but mark my words, you'll want to come back here in a couple of weeks to have another go."

"I doubt it," I said, but feared that he might be right, as he so often was.

"I still think a nice big lawn would look good behind the hotel. We could rig up a net and practise our driving there, and have a smoother bit for putting too."

"I don't think Angela would like that."

"No, she wouldn't, but I'll tell you one thing. If she made the hotel into a place where folk could practise their golf, she'd get a damn sight more customers."

"You're probably right."

He replaced the flag. "I know I'm right. Come on, I'll buy you lunch."

"Lunch is on me," I said, as our round had cost him almost €100 and would have been much dearer had we begun after nine o'clock.

"All right, Alan, you're the boss."

# 17

A few days later, on returning from a spell of grafting at the hotel, I spotted Álvaro watering some plants outside his house, so I jumped out of the car and went to have a word, Zefe having been exiled to the town for a few days.

"Nice plants, Álvaro."

"Hola, Alan. Yes, they were Zefe's idea. He bought them for me at the garden centre."

"He likes coming up here, doesn't he?"

"Ha, if it were up to him he'd never go home."

"Yes, I've sometimes had that feeling too," I said, wondering how best to broach the subject of Zefe maybe one day, in the not too distant future, installing himself in one of his spare bedrooms.

"He loves staying in your annex."

"I know, and as soon as he arrives he comes down to see you, ha ha."

"Yes, he does, ha ha."

We laughed a bit more, and as I laughed I pictured Malcolm's face, which I'd been seeing quite a lot of, because contrary to his avowed intentions he'd been roaming around the hotel like a moody lion, keeping both Gerardo and Malcolm very much on their toes. How would the big man have approached so delicate a subject? I asked myself.

I cleared my throat and gazed into his eyes. "Álvaro, have you ever considered having Zefe as a lodger?"

"As a lodger?"

"Yes, as a lodger."

"Well..."

"On a trial basis at first, of course, just to see how you get on together."

"I..."

"With a view to him maybe moving in permanently."

He opened his mouth again, to no avail.

"That way you'd have more money to buy books, as I'd ensure... I'm sure he'd pay you a decent amount of rent."

I'd hoped that the magic word 'books' would make him see the light, but he continued to shuffle and squirm, struggling to get his head around the idea, I assumed.

"As you know, Zefe is quite old now," I said.

"Yes."

"And he won't be leaving anything to his son, because he never visits him."

"I know. He told me."

"So I believe... did he?"

"Yes, more than once. Alan, he has already dropped many hints about moving in with me, and also about the likelihood of my becoming his heir should I acquiesce to such a move. He's even expressed a preference for that bedroom." He pointed to a dusty first floor window. "And has offered to pay for a thorough cleaning of the house, a skip to take away all my unwanted stuff, and new furniture for the bedroom and whatever else I want." He smiled grimly. "He can be a very persuasive man, Alan."

"I know he can."

"I'm not altogether averse to the idea, and the extra money would indeed be useful, but I'm worried that if he makes the initial monetary contribution that he wishes to, I'll be forever in his debt, so if for whatever reason we cease to see eye to eye, it will put me in an awfully difficult position."

"Yes, I can see that."

"So what do you suggest? Do you have any bright ideas as to how I can allow him to stay, on a trial basis, without compromising myself?"

Malcolm still stood looking over me. "Yes," I said firmly.

"How?"

Malcolm vanished. "I... I'll ask Inma. She's sure to know the best way to go about it."

"Thank you, Alan. Please let me know what she says before Monday, as when I pick him up he'll begin to pressure me once more." He sighed and set down the empty watering can. "How can I concentrate of expounding my ideas if he's constantly looking up at the ceiling through which he sees his proposed bedroom?"

I reassured him that Inma would know what to do, before driving home, kissing her, and succinctly summarising our conversation. Ten minutes later I was knocking on Álvaro's door.

"Ah, Alan."

"Inma wants to know if you're absolutely sure that you want Zefe to come to stay with you. If you're not sure, she suggests that you don't allow him to stay for a single night," I said, before closely observing his reaction as she'd instructed me to.

"Oh, in principle I'm happy for him to come here."

"Are you sure?"

"Yes."

"Good. Then please show me the bedroom."

He led me up the dusty stairs and into the dusty room which was full of old books, files, papers, miscellaneous plastic bags and, scarcely discernible, a few sticks of furniture.

"Is there another spare room?"

"Yes."

"Let's see it."

It was much the same.

"Right, I'll see you tomorrow," I said, before toddling home.

Inma's plan was simple enough and I executed it with Álvaro's help the following afternoon. Within two hours we'd moved all his stuff into the other spare bedroom – which now looked like a clinically certified hoarder's pad – and thoroughly cleaned Zefe's room, including the single bed, chair, small table and enormous wardrobe. As the mattress was a filthy, lumpy monstrosity we carried it to the rubbish bins, before fetching the spare one from the annex.

"This is identical to the one he's been so happy sleeping on, so he should feel at home," I said once we'd plonked it onto the stout bed frame.

"Yes."

"But we'd like it back, eventually."

"Of course." He inhaled vigorously. "It's amazing how different the room looks and smells. So large, so airy, so... different," he said as he paced around.

"Most rooms look more like this one than your other rooms, Álvaro. You ought to think about having a really good clear out, you know."

"Yes, I might."

"So what's the plan regarding Zefe then?"

"Well, rather than driving him up to the annex on Monday, I'll surprise him by bringing him here and showing him the room. That's the first step. I'll have to see if he takes to it."

"Like an old tiger in a new zoo," I thought aloud.

"Ha, yes."

I pictured Zefe prowling around, prodding the tiles with his paw, I mean stick. I shuffled around and found only one loose, right in the corner.

"And if he does take to it?" I said.

He shrugged and a smile played on his lips. "Then he can stay."

"You ought to take him back to town after a few days though."

He stroked his wispy grey beard. "We'll see. Thank you, Alan, and please thank Inma for me, as you've been a great help in turning our idea into reality."

"I'll see you both next week then," I said, and after shaking his hand I scuttled up to the annex, where I collected Zefe's things and left them on the table. All being well, the annex will be ours once more, I hoped, tapping the door after I'd locked it.

It rained on Sunday night, and the next day when Bernie called to tell me that he was preparing his field for planting, I downed tools and drove over. The hotel was all but finished and Arturo and I had been cleaning up, so as I trundled along the lane with the smell of moist earth wafting in through the window, I decided to bill Cristóbal for my invaluable labours and leave the other bits and bats to the regular lads. Apart from a couple of relatively minor jobs, the grouchy builder had nothing lined up and had been pestering me to persuade Malcolm to build a house and/or find him some more rich foreigners. Angela now had a total of eight people for her inaugural course and doubted that many more would sign up, but Malcolm, with whom I'd played pitch and putt twice since our trip to the proper course, seemed serenely optimistic about the success of his wife's debut as a patron of the arts, so I suspected he had something up his sleeve.

For some reason I'd expected Bernie's field to be a hive of activity, but apart from the man himself, I saw only one of his pals from the bar. There was a curious trailer attached to Spartacus, who was positioned in the middle of the field. After jovial greetings Bernie explained that they were digging holes at seven-metre intervals – having measured each row and stuck in canes the previous day – and filling them with water from the tank in the trailer.

"I thought you might like to be present on this monumental occasion," he said.

"Yes, where are the trees?"

"The Garden of Eden wasn't planted in a day, Alan," he said, before switching to Spanish. "Today the holes, tomorrow the trees I get cheap from garden centre."

"This headstrong one should be planting almond trees," said the dark, wiry, weathered but extremely fit man in his sixties who was digging holes very quickly, before bending from the waist to scoop out the loose bits of earth.

"In five years you and me talk, Félix," said Bernie, before filling a bucket from the tank, emptying it into the hole and handing it to me.

So it was that the three of us prepared the field for the following day, when I drove over to help them plant fifty-six tiny olive trees – seven rows of eight – and water them again, after which his friend shook our hands and trundled off in his Berlingo van, which reminded me of Jesús, but first I asked Bernie if he'd paid his pal anything.

"What? Of course not. Us *agricultores* help each other out. We're like a band of brothers. When he needs help I'll be there like a shot."

"Have you seen Jesús lately?"

"Not for a while, but I called him last week. He's got the all clear from the doctors, but he's convinced that the disease is still lurking."

"I suppose it's a good thing to be mentally prepared, in case it returns."

"Hmm, a good thing for him perhaps, but not for others, as he still won't drop the subject. He told me he was barred from the bar for three days. Vicente ordered him to go home and reflect on the error of his ways and only come back if he promised to stop prodding and worrying folk. That's the gist of what he said, anyway. Have you not been to the bar then?"

"Not for a while. I never seem to find the time, although it'd be easy enough to pop in. I must call Juan though, as he's my only real friend there, apart from Vicente himself, but he's usually surrounded by cronies, so you can never have a proper conversation with him." I sighed. "I'm not really a bar person."

"I am, so let's go to your missus's place for a bite to eat."

"Where's Cathy?"

"There." He pointed towards the track. "She's coming to inspect her investment."

I discerned a colourful, fast-moving figure. "What's she wearing?"

"Lycra, I'm afraid. Her yoga's led to a general fitness drive, and a diet, which is why we're having lunch in the bar. I haven't eaten meat for two days."

My sister has always been quite large, but she was looking pretty firm under her skin-tight gear. We strolled over to meet her and I kissed her flushed cheek.

"Been jogging?" I asked.

"No, power walking. Well, the trees look very nice, though I thought they'd be bigger."

"This place is a goldmine, love. Not for nothing do they call olive oil *oro líquido* here."

"Liquid gold, yes, and it's very healthy too."

After enquiring after Inma she powered back towards the house to eat her hummus and salad. That afternoon she would see Doña Elena and then do her yoga, before going for a healthy drink with her classmates, Bernie told me as we walked to the bar.

"It sounds like you're each doing your own thing a lot." I chuckled. "You're not growing apart, are you?"

"No, and it's best not to be under each other's feet all the time. There are a lot of hours in the day when you're retired. It takes some getting used to at first, but we're both pretty busy now. Oh, how's your plot coming along?"

"Er, I dug it over and watered it," I said, not having done anything since then.

"Good. I've done most of my transplanting, but I've saved you a few pots of tomatoes and peppers."

"Thanks, I'll plant them later."

"I've plenty of seeds too."

"I'll plant some then."

"Then give it all a thorough watering."

"Yes."

"Ha, I can tell you haven't got the bug yet, but you will."

"I hope so."

Over lunch I told him about another bug that Malcolm hoped I'd catch.

"Golf, eh? I never took to it myself."

"Malcolm says that all real men get hooked on golf once they've given it a go."

"Well I didn't. It seemed like a daft way to spend a morning to me, chasing a little ball around. All right for folk with nothing better to do, I suppose."

"I just play the odd game of pitch and putt now, to keep Malcolm company, you know."

"Yes, you should keep well in with that one. He really is a goldmine."

On the subject of the hotel he concurred with the big man, saying that though it was a fine place, he doubted that many people would stay.

"Why go there when there are so many interesting and beautiful places to visit? No, those arty courses are their only hope, and I have my doubts about them too. What will your job be?"

"I've no idea. There'll be so many members of staff that I don't really see what I can do."

Bernie gnawed at a pork chop, clearly deep in thought.

"Any suggestions?"

He smacked his lips and wiped them. "As things stand you're in danger of becoming superfluous from the word go."

"I know."

"I can picture you standing there like a spare part, grinning inanely and fidgeting about."

I told him I shared this vision.

"Carrying easels and paint pots and whatnot, and them thinking you're some kind of poor relation drafted in to lend a hand."

"Yes."

"Standing behind them and complimenting their crappy paintings till they tell you to sod off."

"Yes."

"Beaming at them at lunch and wondering what to say."

"Yes, all right, Bernie, I get the picture. What do you suggest?"

He nodded slowly. "I'll just eat this last chop. Brain food, you see."

While he savaged the chop I put my own thinking cap on and imagined how the course members would spend their days. Breakfast, class, practice, lunch, rest, class, practice, stroll, dinner, bed was all I came up with at first, but I swear I was beginning to think along the same lines as Bernie when he finally pushed away his plate.

"They'll want to get out and about," he said.

"Yes, yes," I enthused. "They'll want to go… somewhere, sometime."

"Exactly, and that's where you come in."

"Yes, yes… er, how?"

"You take them."

"Yes. Where?"

"Oh, up the Carche," he said, referring to a highish mountain a few miles to the east. "Or even to the Sierra de la Pila," he added, that being another mountainous area to the south of his house, the place, in fact, where I came a cropper on my mountain bike.

"In my Clio?"

"Course not, you chump. You'll need a minibus… no, too rough for that… a 4×4 with plenty of seats."

I pictured the depleted cornflakes box. "I can't afford to buy one of those."

"Sell some coins."

I pictured my most precious coins and shook my head. "No, I'm not prepared to take such a risk, even assuming Angela agrees with the idea."

"Wimp. If you set up on your own your golf partner would give you a contract, and others might too. You could take folk round the bodegas as well, and… on longer trips to... other pretty places."

"You're starting to sound doubtful, Bern."

He scratched his head. "Well, there are tons more picturesque places in Spain, I suppose. You'd have to set up a business too, which is risky here, as if you don't work you still have to cough up every month. No, you'll have to go for Plan B, which is much simpler."

"Yes. What is it?"

He sighed. "Can you not guess?"

"Er, for Malcolm and Angela to buy the vehicle," I said, quick as a flash.

"That's right."

"I'll drive over afterwards and put it to them."

"No, put it to Malcolm when you're playing golf, just after he's done a good shot."

"I will. Thanks, Bernie. If he agrees, I can be the official driver and take them up all those mountain tracks. They'll like that and I won't feel like a spare part."

Just then Randi stepped behind the bar to ask Inma something, before waving and returning to the kitchen.

"Any more gossip on the Randi front?" I murmured.

"Not really. According to Juan Antonio she's still dallying with the military man, but even when Arvid went to Tenerife to do his altitude training there was no change in their usual pattern."

"Which is?"

"Coffee here, he leaves, she follows, they go off in his car, presumably to his house, then she walks home. The shit'll hit the fan sooner or later though."

"Or their affair might just fizzle out."

"It might. Right, a quick coffee, then back to get your plants."

The first thing I did on returning home with my instant allotment in the boot was to knock on the annex door. Receiving no reply, I unlocked it and saw that Zefe had taken his belongings, so all was going to plan, touch wood, and the old scallywag would soon inform me of his move. I then planted a row of tiny tomato plants, another of peppers, some spinach and melon seeds, and I also stuck in a few small onions that I found in the pantry. After thoroughly watering the whole plot with the hose, I went for a well-deserved shower, feeling a tiny bit more attached to the land.

# 18

On the second of May, the first being a holiday, the hotel was a veritable hive of activity, as all but one member of staff had been called in. They were sixteen strong in the end, Gerardo having decided that he could make do without an assistant manager for the time being, as he intended to turn up every day until things were running smoothly. Sara, the shy girl who Angela and I had interviewed, had great potential, he said, and would be his right-hand woman. He'd also made do with only two kitchen assistants because he insisted that the cooks oughtn't to be above filling the odd dishwasher and suchlike, especially as there'd probably only be eight guests to cater for from the sixth.

"The cooks will be cooking as much for the staff as the guests," Angela murmured glumly as we sat at the back of the neat little dining room where Gerardo was giving his first pep talk. He pranced around like a little Napoleon, telling them that the hotel would be the finest for kilometres around and exhorting them to excel themselves like never before.

"That'll be easy enough with no guests," one young waiter muttered to another, neither of them seeming too impressed by Gerardo's dictatorial posturing, although by observing the body language of the others I perceived that they were listening attentively enough, some no doubt thanking their lucky stars for having landed the easiest jobs of their lives.

Gerardo then handed out their first rotas which included the dates for the various courses some of them were to attend in Elda – kitchen hygiene and suchlike – before sending them off to do their respective tasks with high-pitched words of encouragement.

"He seems to be very organised," I said to Angela as we strolled round to the Hymer.

"He's a real workhorse. Since he finished his last job he's been here every day for God knows how many hours. Thank goodness we got him, or I don't know what on earth we'd have done."

"No, me neither. Where's Arturo today?"

"Not in. He's my employee, remember, and didn't want to come today."

"I thought he'd be keen to meet all the others."

"He is, but I think he wants to set himself apart right from the start," She chuckled. "He doesn't like Gerardo, you see, and will only take orders from me. I expect he'll be in tomorrow."

"It'll be strange not seeing Cristóbal and his lads anymore."

"Yes, and they've done such a good job. Let's see what Malcolm's up to."

Malcolm was up to nothing in the Hymer, as Angela remembered that he'd gone to play golf on the course near Monforte.

She clicked on the kettle. "He'll be back soon, I expect."

Over coffee she told me they were still mulling over the proposal I'd made to him two days earlier in Villena, just after he'd chipped out of a bunker to within three feet of the tee.

"It was clever of you to suggest the 4x4 when he was playing golf, Alan." she said with a smile.

I shrugged. "It just came to me. I think the sight of the grass reminded me of… er, mountains."

"Yes, well, we've discussed it, and while it's a good idea in principle, I've suggested we wait until we see how the first course goes. By then I'll also have an idea how many people will be coming to the second course."

"Oh, what's that one?"

"Creative writing."

"Ah, sounds good. Who will you get to take it?"

"Either a novelist from Dorset or an experimental writer from Hebden Bridge. He tells me that he'll deliver a traditional course, while she favours a more experimental one, pushing them to their limits, she says."

Inevitably I pictured Miguel, Natalia's ex, but shook his bearded image from my head.

"I see. Which is which?"

"The novelist's a man in his fifties, and she's… well, from the photos on her website she looks like some kind of New Age person."

"A hippie?"

"I guess so. I believe there are a lot of folk like that in Hebden Bridge. She's still in her twenties, but is making great waves in the modern writing scene, she says."

Being a conservative soul at heart, I said I thought the novelist chap sounded like the safest bet.

"Yes, but she claims to be able to offer something that he can't."

"What's that? Hubble-bubbles?" I quipped.

"Ha, no, customers. She told me she has quite a following and thinks she might be able to persuade some of them to attend."

"Will they be able to afford it? I mean, don't New Age people try to do without money and… things like that?"

"Well, she says that among her group there are some who are quite well-off. Oh, I don't know what to do. I think I'll wait for the first course to get underway, then make a snap decision."

Faced with the alternatives of the experimental writer with a few groupies or the novelist with no-one at all, I decided not to attempt to sway her either way. The second course was to commence in the middle of June, she said, which seemed like rather short notice to me, but then I had no idea how cheaply she'd sold the first course. Just then a car crunched to a halt on the gravel and Malcolm was soon bounding into the Hymer.

"Ah, Alan, there you are. I thrashed a Czech at matchplay today," he said, looking tanned and pleased with himself.

"A cheque?"

"You know, from Czechoslovakia or whatever the commies used to call it. Mind you, he was a rookie like you, so it was a doddle."

"The staff are here," Angela said while handing him a coffee.

"Good. Ah, Alan, I've got something to give you." He stomped into the bedroom and returned with a brown envelope. "This is from Cristóbal, for services rendered, I think."

"Ah, my pay," I said, though I hoped it also contained my five percent commission for the building job which I'd so adeptly secured for him without doing anything at all.

"It feels a bit thick, eh? He must have slipped you something for getting him the job," he said with a rather grotesque wink.

It didn't feel nearly thick enough to me, but I pocketed it and bade Angela goodbye until the sixth, as I knew that Malcolm would rope me into a game of pitch and putt before then.

"So aren't you coming until then?" she asked me.

"No, I want to take a break and have a think about how I can be of help during the courses. Hopefully I'll arrive full of beans and… ideas," I said, seeing little point in commencing my role of resident spare part until then.

"We'll get you that jeep you asked for soon, Alan," Malcolm said with a grin.

"Will we?" she asked.

"While I was driving back just now I remembered I was in a hire car. Well, I mean, that won't do, will it? We can't be throwing money away like that. So, Alan, if you don't mind picking me up tomorrow at eight, we'll go and have a look for something that'll do for your trips and for us too."

"Great," I said, my motivation multiplying on the spot.

"Yes, we'll get something half-decent that you can drive up them mountain tracks, then pop down to Alicante to drop off the hire car that's costing me a bloody fortune."

"Great."

"Then we'll come back and play a round of that mickey-mouse golf that you like."

"Great."

"Happier now, Alan?" said Angela.

I smiled. "More inspired, yes."

I was happier still when I pulled over in a lay-by and ripped open the envelope. It contained the agreed €10,000 in €500 notes, plus a few paltry fifties for my recent work.

"Put it in the bank, Alan," Inma said when I opened the replenished cornflakes box and dramatically displayed its contents.

"Yes, dear, I will."

"It's not cheap," Malcolm said the following morning on the forecourt of a large car dealership on the outskirts of Elda.

"No, sir, but for a two-year-old car of this type the price is good," said the eager young salesman in English.

"What do you think, Alan?"

"Oh, it's far too posh for my trips up into the mountains, Malcolm. I was thinking of something more like that," I said, pointing at a faded Nissan 4x4 with plenty of seats.

"That? Angela wouldn't be seen dead in that heap, and neither would I." He moved closer. "I mean, it hasn't even got leather seats." He grasped the salesman's arm and led him back to the first car. "No, I'll take this one, but you'll have to knock me a thousand off."

The youngster frowned but his eyes sparkled. "I think we can do that. Will you require finance, sir?"

Malcolm scowled. "Do I look like a bloody pauper?"

"A what, sir?"

"Un pobre," I murmured.

"Ha, no, of course not. When do you wish to take the car, sir?"

"Now," he said, sliding a bank card from his shirt pocket.

It turned out that as Malcolm wasn't yet registered as a resident, he couldn't buy the car.

"What?" his roar echoed around the office. "Is my money no good?"

The chap behind the desk patiently explained that if he or his wife owned property, he could easily arrange residency.

"Oh, I haven't got time to mess about with that now. Put the car in his name then," he said, jerking a thumb in my direction.

"But..." I began.

"Don't worry, you'll soon be making me a present of it."

"All right."

As they insisted on giving the gleaming beast a thorough service, we went to Alicante airport to drop off the hire car. As we drove back in Inma's Ibiza, I reiterated my fears that the new car was just too elegant to drive along stony mountain tracks.

"I might chip the paintwork."

"Don't be soft. Just try not to drive it off a cliff with all Angela's guests inside," he said, before cackling fiendishly, his humour improving as his game of golf – or pitch and putt – drew nearer.

The metallic grey, seven-seater Toyota Land Cruiser was ready when we returned, and after signing the paperwork the man handed me the keys.

"Congratulations," he said to me in Spanish. "May you have health to enjoy it."

"Gracias."

"The car is taxed, but it's customary to have insurance too."

"Ah, yes."

He kindly called an insurance company they worked with and after Malcolm had approved the policy I gave them our details and the man was soon printing out the confirmation they'd emailed to him.

Once outside I proffered the keys.

"You drive it, Alan. If you're going to be up hill and down dale in the thing you'd better get used to it. I'll be on your tail in yours."

Having driven the Hymer, a bit, the Toyota seemed a little less daunting and I was soon gliding up the motorway, marvelling at the smooth ride. I pictured the tracks that I'd mountain-biked along and reasoned that if I took it easy I might not scratch it after all. The guests would be impressed, no doubt, and I looked forward to exploring the routes up the Carche mountain on Inma's next day off. One could get quite used to driving a car like this, I thought as I steered into the golf club car park, and I ought to be grateful that Malcolm had just coughed up €36,000 as if he'd been paying for the weekly shop.

After a quick bite to eat we commenced our double round of the mickey-mouse course and I continued to dwell on the extent of my benefactor's fortune. He must be worth many millions to be able to splash money around like that, I concluded, and I suspected that he wouldn't allow his wife's hotel to fail if she found she enjoyed it as much as she hoped. Still, with no regular guests booked in and only eight for the course, he might be hoping that she'd soon go off the idea.

"Would you consider living in the hotel, if it doesn't take off and Angela decides to call it a day?" I asked him after he'd landed his ball on the green from the fifth tee.

"If I lived in a hotel, I'd live in one in the Bahamas or somewhere," he said as we walked along.

"No, I mean make it into a house again."

"Why so negative, Alan?"

"Oh, I don't mean to be, but like you said, it won't be easy to make a success of it."

"If it isn't, I'll sell it at a profit and clear off somewhere else, unless Angela wants to stay."

"At a profit? Are you sure?"

"Of course I am. We've made a fully functioning hotel for far less than a million. With all the money that's floating around these days that's chickenfeed. Ha, some foreigner would buy it and use it to launder money or turn it into a brothel, or both. When you get as wealthy as I am, Alan, you find you rarely lose out unless you do something really daft. Money begets money, like my granddad used to say."

"Was he a wealthy man?"

"No, he was a small shopkeeper and a lay preacher. Do try to lift the ball this time, Alan."

I lifted the ball, right over the green.

I sighed. "I'm not improving as fast as I thought I would."

"You lack commitment."

"I know," I said, glad that he hadn't bought me all the gear in the end.

"But you keep me company."

"Claro."

"You what?"

"Of course. Do you not fancy learning a bit of Spanish, Malcolm? I could teach you a few things," I said, before describing Bernie's book-free progress from an exponent of the single-word response to a person able to hold a conversation of sorts.

"Oh, I'm sixty-three now. Too old to learn."

I told him why that wasn't the case, but I'll spare you a reprise of my earlier rant.

"Hmm, what's this called then?" he said, raising his putter.

"Putter, I think," I said, pronouncing the word abruptly as a Spaniard would.

"You think?"

"Er, I'm fairly sure. They use a lot of English words in golf, you see, but I'm not really sure when that's just through laziness, or custom, or because the Spanish word doesn't exist."

He held up an iron. "And this?"

I explained that golf clubs in general were called *palos de golf*, and that I thought an iron was a *palo de hierro*, meaning stick of iron.

"You think?" he said with a grin. "I thought you were fluent in Spanish, Alan, or have you been pulling my leg all this time?"

"I'm not fluent yet, but I will be. If I went fishing, for instance, I wouldn't know a lot of the words, but I'd go home and learn them. It's the same with any specific set of vocabulary."

"I was only kidding. How do you say green?"

"They say gren."

"And golf ball?"

"Pelota de golf."

"And bunker?"

"The same."

"And a wood?"

"Palo de madera."

"And fairway?"

"The same, I think."

"Ha, I can tell you're not sure about that one."

"I'll look it up later." (They also say *calle*, as in street, for fairway.)

"Hmm, Spanish doesn't sound as hard as I thought it was."

"Shall I type out a list of useful words and phrases for you?"

"Yes, you do that, Alan. I might give it a go after all."

After the game Malcolm insisted on me driving the Toyota home and promised to take good care of Inma's Ibiza.

"All right, thanks. I'll plan some routes for the guests too," I said, mentally rubbing my hands at the prospect of swanning about in the best car I'd driven since Bernie had allowed me to drive a Bentley owned by the firm he worked for, from the pub to their forecourt, him being over the limit at the time, back in the days when he'd been a sedentary boozehound.

"And don't forget to write my Spanish crib sheet, there's a good lad."

"I won't."


The following day I set off alone to explore the Sierra de la Pila, prior to lunching at Inma and Rosa's bar. I found that I was able to drive all the way up to the radio mast at the top of the mountain without imperilling the paintwork, as long as I steered clear of the odd prickly bush. It was a clear, sunny day and as I viewed the wooded hills and the valley below I felt sure that the budding artists would love to spend some time up there, scribbling away in their drawing pads and soaking up the rays.

"If the Carche is as easy to drive up, I'll have at least two daytrips to offer the guests," I said to Inma when she finally joined me for coffee, having had an especially busy lunch hour. "And if they all want to go, I'll be able to do each trip twice."

"Oh, I'm pleased about that," she said, looking inordinately happy, despite having been rushed off her feet for the last two hours.

"We'll go up the Carche tomorrow and take a picnic, if you like."

"Oh, yes, that would be splendid."

"You seem happy today, love."

"I am. I've got a date for signing the divorce papers at last."

"Oh, when's that?"

"The 23rd of May, a Wednesday."

"So soon?"

"Yes. Oh, I'll feel so glad when it's done."

"Ha, we could get married the very next day," I joked.

"If you like."

My mouth fell open, then I closed it to speak. "Really?"

"Well, maybe not the next day, but whenever you wish. I don't want a lot of fuss though."

I grasped her hand across the table.

"Inma, will you marry me?" I said in English.

"Yes, of course I will." She kissed me quickly, ruffled my hair, and went to serve a customer.

Gobsmacked, I gazed at my coffee as myriad thoughts entered my head at the same time, most of them concerning the wedding. Would she want a really quiet affair with just a couple of witnesses? No, she'd want her parents to be there, but maybe not a big party afterwards. Should we go on our honeymoon straight away or wait for a while? What kind of ring should I buy her, and should I get her an engagement ring too? What would she wear, and what should I wear? Should I rent a limo, or just give the Toyota a good clean, assuming I could still use it, or would Letizia be the best bet, or did it really matter which car we used? Would being married change anything between us? Would our equality before the law – assuming she didn't make any financial stipulations, which I knew she wouldn't – make my feelings of inadequacy return?

I felt a soft hand on the nape of my neck.

"Don't worry about it, Alan. We'll talk about it tomorrow on our picnic. Then we'll both have had time to think about how to go about it. Until then, not a word."

"I want whatever you want."

She put a finger to her lips and entered the kitchen.

# 19

"So," I said at 13.26 hours the following day as we sat on some rocks atop the Carche mountain, gazing at the flatlands around Jumilla and the cordilleras beyond. "Have you decided how you'd like it to be?"

"I have certain preferences, if that's what you mean."

"Go on."

"Well, I'd like it to be on a Saturday morning, so that my parents can come, have lunch with us, then drive back to Murcia without too much traffic. It'll be easier for Natalia too. Rosa's going to have a word with her Uncle Alberto, who's on the council, to see if that's possible. If it is, I don't mind which Saturday it is, but I'd prefer it to be sooner rather than later, to please my parents."

"On Saturday the… 26th of May then, if we can?"

"Yes, if we can."

"What will you wear?"

"Nothing special. That lime green dress maybe."

"What should I wear?"

"Whatever you want."

"I don't have a tie."

"Then don't wear one, or borrow one."

This I took to be a hint that I should dress fairly smartly, with a tie, but not necessarily in a suit.

"I'll buy you an engagement ring soon."

"No, please don't. I only wear this ring my grandmother gave me and I don't wish to be quizzed about the wedding at work."

"And a wedding ring?"

She chuckled. "If you like we'll buy matching bands."

"Yes, I'd like that. Oh, if someone had told me when I stepped off the plane in Alicante that I'd be getting married to a beautiful Spanish woman within little over a year, I'd have said they were crazy." I put my arm around her. "I'm a lucky man."

"And I'm a lucky woman. Come on, before we eat let's have a wander round and find some good places to draw from."

"Good idea. Next week I'll be up here with them."


We had a pleasant lunch, well wrapped up at a touch over the height of Ben Nevis, before driving happily home, so when Juanca called at half past five I'd just woken up after a most pleasant siesta. I ignored the call and phoned him back half an hour later.

"Did you call?" I said abruptly, suspicious that he'd got in touch with me so soon after I'd received my commission from his cousin, which he'd once suggested he deserved a chunk of.

"Yes, I did. How have you been keeping, Alan?" he said in a suspiciously upbeat voice.

"Not bad. And you?"

"Oh, you know, plodding on and paying the bills, ha ha."

"Ha ha. How can I help you, Juanca?"

"I just thought we might meet up sometime soon."

"What for?"

"Oh, one should keep in touch, you know. I'd hoped you might drop by my office, but you haven't, so I called you."

"Well, it's nice to hear from you, but I'm quite busy at the moment."

"All right, maybe another time then."

"Yes." I softened a tiny bit. "Yes, I'll call in one day and you can buy me a coffee."

"Of course, or lunch."

"Yes. Goodbye then."

"Goodbye… oh, I almost forgot to tell you something." He paused for effect.

"Go on."

"Now, what was it? Ah, yes, a Frenchman called in to ask about buying a house in the area."

"That's good."

"Yes, he arrived in a big Volvo with French number plates, so I knew he was French rather than Belgian."

"Well spotted."

"Yes, and he said that someone had recommended me as the best estate agent in the area."

"How nice."

"Ha, the trouble was that his accent was so strong that I couldn't distinguish the name very well. It sounded like Alain, but I can't be certain."

Surer than ever that he was after a share of the commission, which he would attempt to wangle out of me after giving me some cock and bull story about this Frenchman, I told him that if he wasn't sure, he needn't worry too much about it.

"Oh, but I must find out who this Alain is, Alan. My impeccable reputation depends on me always honouring my promises to my unofficial agents."

"Do you know any Alains?"

"Not that I recall, Alan. Alas, the man was in a hurry, so I couldn't ascertain how or where he'd come across this Alain, but I thought you might be able to shed some light on the matter."

"I don't think so," I said, before Malcolm's fearsome face appeared in my mind's eye. He warned me not to allow my sadly underdeveloped commercial instincts to let an opportunity pass me by, and he also scorned my fear of Juanca bamboozling me out of part of my commission. All this occurred in half a second, and in the other half I swore that whatever he said, not a cent of Cristóbal's money would be up for grabs. "Although he might have meant Alan, of course."

"Ah, yes, he might have meant Alan."

"Look, I was coming into town anyway, so I'll call round."

"Yes, you do that. I shall await you with open arms, Alain, I mean Alan."

As soon as Inma stepped out of the shower, I enveloped her in a towel.

"Oh, thanks. Is this what married life is going to be like?"

"Yes, I shall be your slave," I said, before drying her a bit while asking if a Frenchman had been in the bar, asking about houses.

"Yes, a couple of days ago. I gave him one of your cards."

"Ah, why didn't you tell me?"

"Oh, we often give them to foreigners who express interest in the area."

"I bet he showed it to the rascal," I muttered. "But how would my card lead him to Juanca?"

She sighed and shook her turbaned head. "Because we tell them where to go, of course. He didn't seem so interested, so I thought no more of it."

I told her about Juanca's call and my fear that it was a ruse to prise my hard-earned cash away from me.

"Be firm with him. Imagine what he'd have done if Cristóbal had stated clearly that he didn't wish you to have a share."

"I will. I'll be firm. Thank you, dear."

"Nice motor, Alan," the impious agent said after trotting outside.

"Oh, it's all right. So, tell me about this Frenchman who Inma gave one of my cards to."

"Not so fast, Alain, ha ha. I'll lock up and we'll go to the bar. We have a lot of catching up to do."

Over coffee he peppered me with questions, mainly about the hotel, which I answered briefly until we got onto my future job there, which I embellished somewhat.

"…so that's what the Toyota's for, you see. I'll be taking the guests on trips and generally entertaining them," I concluded after droning on for some time about my key role.

"I see, but rumour has it that the staff there have very little to do."

"They're training and… things."

"But I believe only one small group of people are booked in, to do some kind of course."

I wondered who the blabbermouth could be, but there was no law against talking about one's job, and others would ensure that the any news soon reached Juanca's ears.

"Yes, well, these things take time."

"And will they pay you for driving people around and… things?"

"Of course."

He sighed. "Oh, Alan, I don't see much future for you at the hotel, not when there are twenty more people working there."

"There are nowhere near so many," I snapped. "That's idle gossip. Anyway, I didn't come here to talk about that, but first tell me what you've been up to. You never speak about yourself."

He limply swatted the air. "Oh, my life is very dull. I come here, show people houses, then go home."

"Hmm."

"Although I have separated from my wife and am living in a small flat in Jumilla."

"Oh, I'm sorry to hear that. What happened?"

"She claims that I've paid her no attention for years, but the real reason she wants a divorce is because she's been seeing another man, a mere office worker, younger than her." He shrugged and wiped his eye, though I'd discerned no tears.

"Oh, I'm sorry."

"He's after the money he knows she'll be entitled to. He's fat, like her, and lazy, like her. They make a good couple and I hope they'll soon eat themselves to death with the... small amount of wealth I've acquired by working so hard for so long."

"But you'll keep half of it, won't you?"

"If I'm lucky, but she's trying to keep the house, so I'll have to buy a new one and... oh, you don't want to hear about my trifling worries, Alan," he said with a brave smile.

I sighed, shook my head, and cunningly perused his wedding ring finger. There was no ring and no mark. Could he be telling the truth, or was it a ruse to enlist my sympathy before browbeating me out of five grand?

"How's your daughter?" I asked.

"Still in Stockholm, but she has been home twice to comfort her lonely old father." He sighed sadly, before pushing back his cuffs and leaning over the table. "Anyway, enough about that. I teased you on the phone about the Frenchman, but it's true that he showed me your card, so we must talk business. Drink up and we'll return to the office."

The office was as scruffy as it had been before our rapid clean-up some months earlier.

"So, this Frenchman is a rather cunning kind of man and he appears to be well-off. He's no fool and has a clear idea of what he wants."

"What's that?"

"He wishes to buy one of the many unfinished chalets around here, with plenty of land. Some belong to local people who ran out of money because of the crisis, others to ruined builders, and a few are already in the hands of the banks. I know most of the owners, but the sale won't make us much money, as the price will be cheap, so it's imperative that we also contract the builder for the Frenchman."

"Right, but where do I come into it?"

"That depends. You'll get your five percent for the sale anyway, as it was through you that he came here."

"Through Inma, but yes," I said, glad that I hadn't told him we were going to be married.

"Yes, because I honour my promises, Alan."

"Yes, so do I," I said, giving him a steely, not-to-be-trifled-with look.

"Yes, but some don't, like my cousin."

"That's debatable, Juanca. I mean, if everyone got a commission for everything, there wouldn't be much to go round, would there?"

He rapped the desk. "*I* sold that house to that great big Englishman. With no sale there would have been no building. We worked together for years, then he let me down."

"Hmm."

"First him, then my wife. Am I such a despicable person, Alan?" he said, the film of moisture on his eyes caused by Cristóbal's treachery, I suspected.

"No, you aren't. Ha, you can get your revenge by not giving Cristóbal the work on the Frenchman's house, if he buys."

"He will buy, but I don't want revenge, Alan. I wish to heal the wounds caused by his unthinking greed."

"Do you?"

"Of course. He is family, after all."

"Yes, I guess he is."

"And what will he do now, eh? I know for a fact that he has only two trifling jobs lined up, and what then? And it's not only that... him who I'm thinking of. What will his workers do? How will they put food on their families' tables? Are their children to go to school clothed in tattered rags?"

I raised my hands. "All right, all right, I've got the message. Is there anything I can do to help heal the wounds?"

"Yes, Alan, there is."

"Then tell me what it is and I'll do it."

His lips curled up a bit. "But will you have the tact and subtlety required for such a delicate task?"

"Yes, I'll... if you give me some idea of how to go about it," I said, having resisted a strong impulse to tell him that I'd ask Inma.

He smiled. "It's quite simple really. Lead up to it however you like, but tell him that as soon as he appears here with €5000 in cash, he will once more become my number one builder."

I stroked my chin and gulped. Five grand was the amount he probably thought I ought to pay him, so did he expect me to capitulate rather than risk being ridiculed by Cristóbal? Ha, I was made of sterner stuff than that.

"Right, I'll call him later."

"No, please see him face to face, as I want you to see how he reacts to my generous offer."

"Er, how is it a generous offer, Juanca?"

"Because it ought to be ten, and if he doesn't want a firm from out of town to build the Frenchman's chalet, he'd better pay up, because we all know that Malcolm has no intention of building another house."

"Do we? Do you?"

"Of course. It stands to reason. They have that large motorhome to live in, and if the hotel fails, they won't wish to live there."

"Er, what makes you say that?"

"Simple intuition."

"Ah."

He grinned. "And a conversation overheard by... someone."

"Fran?" I said, referring to the first waiter we'd interviewed, but his face remained placid.

"It's not important. I have eyes and ears everywhere. So, will you tell my cousin what he must do?"

"Yes."

"Should he prove hostile to my suggestion, remind him how many jobs I've secured for him over the years. Simple men like him have a tendency to ignore the bigger picture when they're temporarily blinded by greed, but I feel sure that he'll see reason if you approach the subject in the right way. Besides, I'd rather work with him than others. I know he's a good builder and the well-being of my customers is of paramount importance to me."

"Yes, Juanca."

He stood up and leaned over his desk. "And you, Alan, should also think of the future. What can the hotel offer you?"

"I..."

His stare intensified. "I'll tell you. At best a mediocre job, and at worst nothing at all. Sell your coins and work with me. Above all work with me, because the European economy is picking up, there are hundreds of houses standing empty, and thousands of foreigners who want to buy them. You *know* it makes sense, Alan."

Wilting somewhat under the heat of his fiery eyes, I told him I'd go to see Cristóbal right away, but that I didn't hold out much hope.

"Tell him not to bring €500 notes. Even the banks don't like them."

As I drove to Cristóbal's chalet I found myself chuckling softly. I had to admit that it had been fun to listen to Juanca's greed-driven eloquence again and I didn't feel averse to working with him now and then, especially when I considered how little I'd have to do. I wondered why he was so keen to have me back on board and concluded that it was simply because I was a calm man of trustworthy appearance who spoke Spanish. Whether I'd be any good as a tour guide, I didn't know, but – laying modesty aside for a moment – I did have a certain indefinable something when it came to putting people at their ease and persuading them to buy a property. Some folk succumb to the hard sell, but of the many who don't, quite a few seem to like my approach, I was telling myself when the builder's fine house came into view and I remembered my onerous errand.

I pressed the intercom button and no sooner had the automatic gate begun to slide open than he came striding out, still dressed in his work clothes.

"So your boss has still got plenty of cash to splash about, has he?" was his greeting as I opened my door.

"Hola, Cristóbal. I've just been talking to your cousin Juanca."

"It's time Malcolm began to think about the house I'm going to build for them."

"Juanca asked me to come here to see you."

"Tell him that I can do the work this summer if we prepare the plans now. Otherwise I'll end up building for someone else."

"Are you listening to me, Cristóbal?"

"Are you listening to *me*?"

"Yes, but you'd better listen to me, as Malcolm has no intention of building a house there at all."

He scowled especially fiercely to hide the effects of this crushing blow, I deduced.

"I can guess why my damn cousin has sent you. He daren't come here as he knows I'd set the dogs on him."

I observed the two spaniels sniffing around by the fence. "Yes, Cristóbal. Er, why do you think he's sent me here?"

"Because he wants me to pay him ten thousand. He knows the work is over and he thinks it's time to pressure me, but I won't back down."

"Thanks for my envelope, by the way."

He grunted.

"Juanca told me that a wealthy Frenchman is about to buy an unfinished chalet and wishes to contract a builder to finish it."

He began to lick his lips, but whipped his tongue in and clamped his mouth shut.

"Juanca only wants you to give him five thousand, then the job will be yours."

"Ha, another job that you'll both want a commission for."

I stood firm. "Yes, but it's only ten percent." I subtly puffed out my chest. "Juanca will sell the Frenchman the house and I'll personally convince him that you're the builder for the job. I'll take him round the hotel and show him the finer points of your workmanship," I said with suitably forthright gestures.

"Yes, yes, I'm sure you will. Tell him that when the new building contract is signed, I'll hand over the five thousand."

"Will you?"

"Of course. Do I look stupid?"

"No, but why not give it to him now as a gesture of good faith?"

"Have you met the *gabacho*?" he asked, referring to the Frenchman.

"No, but Inma has," I said, remembering that she'd said he hadn't seemed all that interested. "But do what you think best."

"Tell him what I said. I'm going for a shower. Adiós."

"Adiós, Cristóbal."


"Ha, I expected nothing less of the stubborn devil," Juanca said back at the office. "Thank you, Alan. It's good to have you both back in the fold."

Rather than baaing, as the expression is the same as in English, I remembered my inspired and inspiring words. "Yes, and I'll personally convince the Frenchman that Cristóbal is the builder for the job. I'll take him round the hotel and show him the finer points of his workmanship," I said with even greater finesse the second time around.

"Yes, Alan," he said, looking amused, as I think I'd overdone it and had sounded a bit like Laurence Olivier in *Richard III* when he'd mislaid his horse.

"Let me know when you need me, Juanca."

"I will, but I also need you to find me more buyers."

"After the course at the hotel I'll begin to look," I said, as a married man must pull his weight.


"Juanca says he's glad that I'm back in the fold," I told Inma over dinner.

She baaed softly.

"That's what I thought."

"It's good though."

"I know. It's tough work, but someone has to do it."

"Have you spoken to Beth lately?"

"No, but I will, right after dinner."

Beth told me that Bill's funeral had been a dignified affair and that two of his daughter's servants had helped to bear the coffin from the village church to the graveyard, the other bearers being nephews.

"It was like stepping into another world, Alan, like one of those costume dramas. I'm glad I went now. Everyone was really nice, as they knew how well we got on together."

"And how well you looked after him. He was a grand chap, wasn't he?"

"Yes, he was. I'm keeping my eyes open for the spring arrivals, by the way. I'll let you know as soon as someone wants to take a look inland."

"Thank you, Beth."

"This resurrection of my house-selling career has been rather sudden," I said later in bed.

"That's what it's like, I guess. It's just a question of keeping one's eyes open."

"Like you did with the Frenchman."

"Yes. Bonne nuit, mon chéri."

"Bonne nuit, ma chérie."

# 20

"Alan, I have some amazing news," Angela blurted down the phone the following morning at half past eight, which was most unlike her.

"Morning, Angela. What is it?"

"Some *guests* arrived at the hotel yesterday evening," she gushed.

"Oh, did they come early for the course?" I asked, it being due to start the next day.

"No, no, I mean real guests."

"Oh, aren't the course guests real guests?"

"No, yes... no, because I lured them here with special rates. These proper guests just came across the place and liked the look of it. There are *four* of them, Alan, two couples, and they're staying for four whole nights, so for a short while we'll have fourteen guests staying. We'll be practically full. Isn't that exciting?"

"Yes, it is, but how come it's fourteen?"

"Well that's another bit of good news. Two more people signed up for the course a couple of days ago. Isn't it wonderful?"

"It's great, Angela," I said, trying to match her enthusiasm, which wasn't easy, as I didn't feel much. Juanca's warning that the hotel was unlikely to put much bread on my table had hit the mark and I'd woken up in a sombre state of mind regarding my limited duties there.

"As there are ten people on the course, you'll have to take them out in two groups."

"Oh, yes, so I'll have at least four outings," I said, instantly bucking up.

"Unless only six want to go."

"Ah, that's true," I said, my morale falling again, as I'm a sensitive man first thing in the morning.

"It was such a good thing that Gerardo was here when the couples arrived, Alan. Without him we'd have been in a tizzy, but he knew what to do right away."

"Yes, well, he is a hotel manager, isn't he?"

"Yes, but I wasn't even sure if we were prepared for guests. It turned out that we had everything we needed to give them a good dinner, even fresh bread. It was simply masterful the way he organised everybody. He really is on the ball."

I held the phone at arm's length and imitated Gerardo's sycophantic smile.

"Alan, are you there?"

"Yes."

"I said Tina's arriving later."

"Ah, good. Is she one of the course guests?"

She tutted. "No, the teacher. Will you be able to come over and meet her?"

I'd rather hoped to spend Inma's day off with her, so I asked her what time Tina would be arriving.

"Some time this afternoon."

"Then I'll be over by six."

"All right." She chuckled. "Are you not curious to know where the unexpected guests are from?"

I shook my head. "Yes, where are they from?"

"From East Anglia, of all places. They were just touring around and came across us. When they saw the hotel they couldn't resist staying. It's a good sign, isn't it?"

It's uncanny, I thought. "Yes, it is," I said.

"Anyway, I must go to make sure they're all right."

I imagined Sybil from Fawlty Towers, perched on the edge of their breakfast table, chattering away, but no, Angela was nothing like her. Her hair wasn't permed for a start.

"I'll see you later, Angela."

"Bye, Alan."


"But they feel warm to me," Inma said after crouching to feel my sandalled feet.

"It's an expression. It means to not feel very keen about something."

"And what is it that you don't feel keen about?"

"Oh, meeting the teacher, then meeting the participants tomorrow morning. I always feel nervous when I'm about to meet people, and I think someone in my role ought to be enthusiastic, like a... red coat."

"A soldier?"

"Er, something like that," I said, not wishing to explain the joys of Butlins just then.

She grasped my arms and gave them a shake. "Just be yourself and everything will be fine. What does it matter, after all? And you'll get to drive them around in the Toyota. You'll enjoy that, won't you?"

I agreed that I would, as long as none of my passengers proved tiresome or carsick.

"But I'd like my Ibiza back, so please leave the Toyota there today."

As the morning was sunny and warm, we decided to spend some time on the new patio, having rarely ventured up there. A pleasant breeze tempered the sun's rays and I'd just concluded that all was right with the world after all when I spied Zefe clumping up the track. Although it was about time he showed his face, I wasn't especially eager to entertain him just then, but I needn't have worried, because he just hulloed us from below, waving his stick in the air.

"How's it going, Zefe?" I said, leaning over my splendid railings.

"Good, good, I've just come to tell you that I'm fine. Hola, Inma."

"Hola, Zefe. Are you settling in?"

"Yes, I am. Such a nice room with views to the south. I get the sun all day, unlike in there, where it was chilly until the afternoon."

"That's because it was mostly winter, Zefe," I pointed out.

"Yes, my room's marvellous, but the house is a mess. I've told Álvaro that we must get a skip and throw a lot of things out, then give the place a good clean."

I groaned, sure that he wouldn't hear me.

Inma tittered and prodded my calf with her bare foot. "I'll give you the number of a good cleaner, Zefe. She'll come up for a day and clean the whole place, as soon as you've got rid of all the junk."

"Yes, please do, Inma."

"Once you've got the skip I'll come and give you a hand," I said, Inma's quick thinking having hopefully spared me irksome cleaning duties. "But I won't clean," I added, just to be on the safe side.

"Of course not, Alan. You've done enough, and we're very grateful. Álvaro isn't a bad cook, but his idea of tidiness is lamentable."

I sniggered at the audacity of the man. "Are you paying him rent, Zefe?"

"Not rent, as such, but I'm making a handsome contribution."

"Good."

"I'm not as poor as I appear to be, Alan."

"I know."

"And when God calls me to his side, many years from now, you'll find that I haven't forgotten your kindness."

The devil's side, more like. "Yes, Zefe."

"Can we have the mattress back sometime?" said Inma.

"Yes, I've already ordered a bigger bed. I always found the bed in the annex a little uncomfortable, but I didn't like to complain. I'll be off now."

"Yes, look after yourself and give our regards to Álvaro," I said, sensing the end of an era.

"I will."

"Bye, Zefe."

"Bye. Oh, when are we going swimming, Alan?"

I laughed. "Not this week, I'm afraid, but definitely next week."

"All right, Alan."

We watched him plod down the track until he turned the corner onto his new street.

I chuckled. "What an old scoundrel he is."

"Yes, but he's come a long way since you met him."

I remembered his foul-mouthed outburst when I first entered his crummy flat, and his fears that social services would confine him to a home, as he'd seemed just about ready for one.

"If you can do what you've done with Zefe, just imagine how easy dealing with a few mature art students will be."

"A piece of cake," I said in English.

"Child's play," she responded.

"Easy-peasy. A walk in the park. I can't wait." I took her hand and sighed. "But I still don't want to go."

I needn't have worried, or not much, because Tina, the course leader, was a charming woman of about my own age from Cheshire. She dressed casually, not in an especially arty way, and had been doing similar courses for years. I'd have liked to have shown her around and suggested the best places for drawing and painting, but the ever-present Angela usurped that role, so I just tagged along, murmuring inanities now and then. When she retired to her first-floor room for a rest, Angela trotted off to check the other rooms, so I wandered down to reception and found the ever-present Gerardo behind the desk, looking like a second-rate male model on his day job.

"Hello, Alan, how are you?"

"Muy bien. Y tu?"

"Very well, thank you. Making sure that everything is prepared for tomorrow."

"Yes, I'm looking forward to meeting the guests," I lied in Spanish.

"Don't worry about them, Alan. My team is ready to receive them."

"Bien. Hasta luego."

"See you later, Alan."

Fecking prick, I thought, as I'm not one for swearing much, even in my head.

On my aimless wander around the ground floor I was fortunate enough to come across Arturo, looking very much the maintenance man cum caretaker cum chauffeur cum gardener, with a huge bunch of keys hanging from his belt and an array of pens in the pocket of his black canvas jacket. His glossy hair was tied smoothly back and I saw that a cap wouldn't suit him.

"Hola, Arturo. So many keys already?"

"Most of them are mine. I used to find them useful in my old life, but I think they make me look official and important."

"Ha, yes, they do."

"Will you be leaving the Toyota?"

"Yes. Why do you ask?"

"Oh, my old van is too scruffy to use, you see, so I've parked it around the back."

"I see. Er, where do you have to go?"

"Well, I have to pick up two of the guests from the airport at about half past one in the morning. Most of them will make their own way here, but Angela asked me to go to get them, as it's so late."

I should have stomped off to find her and tell her that *I* would collect the guests, as it was *my* job to transport them, but I somehow didn't fancy getting home in the middle of the night, so I just nodded. He might have sensed my annoyance, because he then told me that he'd been assigned a little room behind the kitchen.

"Mainly for when I finish really late. I don't mind staying, as it keeps me out of the bars, and I'll make sure I get time off to see my Rocío." He smiled. "I hope to work a lot of hours at first, because we don't really know how long this is going to last, do we?"

"No," I said, before remembering my other more dynamic hat and putting it on. I felt taller. I popped my head through the door to make sure no-one was eavesdropping. I cleared my throat. "I... er, have reason to believe that your old friend Cristóbal will get a big job soon. A... certain person wishes to have a chalet built and

I'm going to... that's to say, someone is going to ensure that he gets the contract, so it might be in your interests to stay in touch with him," I tapped my nose. "Eh?" I added for effect, gazing down at him like a kindly Victorian schoolmaster.

"That's good to know, Alan."

I shrugged. "Oh, one wants the best for one's friends, you know."

"But if you're still pulling strings regarding that sort of thing, what are you messing about here for?" he said, or words to that effect.

I handed him the Toyota keys to add to his collection. "I don't know, Arturo, I really don't know."


"The trouble with that damn Gerardo being such a pillock and speaking English to me is that I can't get involved in anything," I moaned to Malcolm in the Hymer.

"What do you want to get involved for? Hotel work's for lackeys, Alan. Drive the arty buggers wherever you feel like going and leave the women's work to the others. That's what they're paid for."

"Yes, but I'd hoped to have a bigger role and get paid too."

"You'll be paid for swanning about with them, and handsomely. I'll see to that. We can't have you short of a bob or two, can we?"

Businessmen like Malcolm must be masters of psychological manipulation, because I bit the bait like a starving perch. I pushed myself up on the comfy seat, entwined my fingers, and stuck out my chin.

"Malcolm, it's not that I *need* to work here, as I have more irons in the fire. It's just that I expected to feel more involved, that's all. You know, after all the building and the... build-up, to find myself out in the cold is a bit... well, belittling."

His mocking gaze helped me to relax my silly posture.

"If you want I can have you kitted out in a waiter's uniform before you can say knife, lad."

"I..."

"You can't be a receptionist because you haven't got a degree in tourism."

"Er..."

"So, you'll work seven till four on some days and four till twelve on others, and get a weekend off about once a month."

"Yes, but..."

"Within a year or so, if you prove to be better than all the others, you might be promoted to head waiter. How does that sound?"

I hung my head. "Rubbish."

"Exactly, so no more nonsense about working here. Sell your coins and houses and treat this as a bit of a lark that you get paid for."

"Yes, Malcolm."

"Where's my crib sheet?"

"Oh, I forgot to do it."

"Ha, some waiter you'd make. Pitch and putt on Wednesday."

"I might have to take them out."

"I'll pick you up at eight; you and the crib sheet."

"Yes, Malcolm."

"Here are your car keys."

"Thanks. We'd better change the name on the Toyota soon."

"Think on what I've said, and don't be a bloody loser."

"No, Malcolm." I stood up. "Adiós."

"Adio-ows," he said, so I knew I'd need to work on his pronunciation.

# 21

Often when you worry about things and then they turn out all right, you wonder why you wasted all that mental energy worrying about them in the first place. It happens to me a lot, as you'll have gathered, but when I met the participants of the art course at midday on Sunday I saw straight away that they'd be no bother. Their ages ranged from about forty to seventy – seven women and three men – and when I gave them my little spiel in the dining room they all listened attentively. I told them I was in charge of excursions and had planned two scenic half-day trips which they were welcome to come along on. They would take place on the Monday and the Tuesday, morning and afternoon if numbers were high, and I'd also be available if they wished to expand their horizons in any particular direction on Thursday, Friday and Saturday, Wednesday being reserved for golf, I said with a charming chuckle.

"Golf, you say?" said one chap of about sixty.

"Er, I meant that I was playing. It's my day off, you see."

Angela, who stood smilingly by my side, unable to leave me even these few rays of limelight, must have assessed the tall, bald, tanned man in an instant, as she recklessly suggested that he might want to join Alan and her husband in a relaxing game of golf.

"I'd love too. I've sort of tagged along with my wife, you see, to have a go at drawing, but I wouldn't be averse to playing a round. You don't mind, do you dear?" he said, not to me, but to the placid lady by his side.

"Of course not, John. If Alan's all right with that."

"It's only pitch and putt actually," I said, glancing nervously at Angela, who I assumed was still in her right mind. I mean, Malcolm wanted nothing whatsoever to do with the guests, so had his wife just put my foot in it?

"I don't mind pitch and putt. I'm not much of a player anyway."

I nodded feebly. "So," I said, clapping my hands and smiling stiffly. "Who's up for my first excursion? Not the golf, but the mountain, as the golf is an extra for this lucky gentleman, ha ha," I said, feeling like Basil Fawlty in one of his pickles. I know it's a bit naff to refer repeatedly to a TV series, but you must remember that having been a stay-at-home sort of man for most of my life, ninety percent of my hotel experience had come from watching Fawlty Towers. I'm also tall, gangly and of a nervous disposition, so the comparison isn't without foundation.

Five of them were definitely up for at least one excursion, four were maybes, and one lady had only come to draw and paint with the teacher's guidance, so I guaranteed the five keen ones a pew at 9.00am the following day and said that we'd take things from there.

"Do you have any questions or suggestions or... anything?" I said.

They hadn't, so Angela steered me out as Tina entered with a large folder and a supremely confident smile on her face.

"Er, was that a good idea, Angela?"

"What?"

"Inviting that man along to golf, with Malcolm."

"Oh, yes," she said as we walked outside into the sunshine. "The lawns are looking better now, aren't they?"

"Yes, er…. would you mind telling Malcolm that the man's coming along? I'd rather it came from you."

"Alan."

"Yes?"

"Malcolm goes to Monforte and plays with whoever he finds there."

"That's true."

"He isn't an ogre."

"No."

"He's a gregarious man when he wants to be."

"Yes."

"And it might be in your interests to take John along."

"Why? Because he probably isn't as bad as me?"

She stopped and faced me. "There is that, as Malcolm's a bit disappointed that you haven't got keener, but there's something else, probably nothing, but it pays to follow these things up."

"What things?"

"John and Susan are the guests who Arturo picked up last night."

"Ah."

"So they were at breakfast this morning, logically."

"Yes."

"I had a little chat with them (vision of Sybil F.) and it turns out that they're thinking about retiring to a warmer country. It's just an idea at present, but one that you could follow up on the golf course. Do you see now?"

"Yes, thank you, Angela."

"If nothing else it'll give you a bit of practice. Let's face it, hotel work isn't your thing, so you ought to hone your house selling skills. Malcolm will probably give you a few pointers too, as he could sell sand to the Arabs."

I bridled a bit at her aspersion that I couldn't hack it in the hotel world. She must have noticed.

"Alan, as this project has slowly come to fruition there have been many turning points where decisions have had to be made, by me, by you, by other people," she said in an ominously schoolmarmish voice.

"Hmm."

"At each of the points that concerned you, you've backed away from responsibility."

"I..."

"Please let me finish," she said, patting my arm. "When we first bought the place I could well imagine you becoming the manager, had you been willing to prepare yourself for the job, but I soon saw that you didn't have the drive or the inclination to do that. Since then you've been edging yourself away little by little, until in the end I thought you might not even want to take them on trips in the splendid car that Malcolm's bought for the purpose."

"But..."

"I'm not criticising you, Alan."

"Oh, that's good to hear."

She chuckled and patted my arm again. "No, I understand it perfectly. As Malcolm has pointed out to me, why would a man who can make good money just by introducing one person to another want to slave away like a Chinaman in a sweatshop? They're his words, by the way."

"I suppose there's some truth in what you say."

"I've told you this for your own good, Alan."

"Yes."

"With this man John, and others like him, you must use your quiet charm to steer him around to the subject of houses, then subtly hint that this area is a good one and... well, you know the rest. Not everyone can do that, Alan, but I saw that you had that ability when Malcolm and I came over, and if you can sell a house to him, you can sell one to anybody."

I shrugged modestly.

"And with Malcolm with you on Wednesday, the poor man hasn't got a chance. Now, it'll be lunchtime soon, so will you eat with us and get to know the guests, or will you go home?"

"Er, it's Inma's first full weekend off for ages, so… er..."

"You see?"

"Yes, I see."

"Do come for breakfast at eight tomorrow though, then you can sort out the trips."

I smiled and nodded. "Oh, yes, I'll be here at eight, if not before."

She shook her head and smiled. "You are funny, Alan. Hasta mañana."

"Hasta mañana, Angela," I said, before trudging off to my Clio, but I soon cheered up, as every word she'd said had been true and on Wednesday I'd be working my wizardry on John, touch wood.

The next morning I drove the five most eager trippers slowly up the wide but rather rough track to the top of the Carche mountain. It was a dull, breezy day down below, but blowing a gale on the mountain, so after standing around like disconsolate penguins for a few minutes, we clambered back into the Toyota and I suggested driving into town for a look around and a coffee. On hearing their lukewarm murmurs of assent I ought to have enthused like a seasoned Redcoat about the churches, the pretty old streets, the wide avenue and the buzzing hostelries, but I had to concentrate on the descent and by the time we were back on tarmac a pregnant silence had descended on the company. Pregnant with what, I didn't know, but try as I might I couldn't manage to utter more than the occasional banality, until the polite lady by my side pointed out a 'Se Vende' sign and asked if it meant that the tumbledown house was for sale.

I confirmed that it did, before gradually and involuntarily launching into what turned into a shameless sales pitch regarding all the wonderful properties one could buy at knock-down prices, due to Spain's slow recovery from the economic crisis... and on I droned until a man in the back asked me if I sold houses for a living.

"Oh, not exactly, but I have been known to introduce people to... er, other people and help them to... ooh, look, here we are. The town looks a bit scruffy and modern from here, but there are some lovely old buildings that haven't been pulled down yet, and a nice market, though it's not on today."

"Are there any good places for drawing?" asked a stout, red-faced lady impatiently.

"Yes, there's... let me see..." I began, but for the life of me I couldn't think of any more picturesque spots than the town hall square, occupied by a small roundabout around which traffic constantly circled, so I dropped them off near the bar terrace and went off to find somewhere to park, no easy task in a town where little provision had been made for parking since the 1960s, I guessed, as it's always been more profitable to build flats than car parks. As I toured the one-way system of narrow streets I recalled the day when I'd bought my mountain bike from Arturo in Vicente's bar and then ridden the wrong way along one such street. Ah, such days of innocence and discovery! Now here I was, stressed out in a huge car, attempting to park before joining my charges, who would probably be standing around like disconsolate ducks, waiting to berate me for wasting their precious morning.

In the event I needn't have worried, again, as I found them seated around a terrace table, drinking coffee and chatting away like old friends, having bonded easily in my absence, so I slipped into the spare chair, ordered a *cortado*, and did what I do best in company; namely beam, nod, chuckle and throw in the odd monosyllabic comment. One lady soon trotted off down the street to sketch a church she'd spotted, while another had a go at the fountain in the middle of the roundabout. Then a portly chap happily began to draw an ancient Seat 600, before getting annoyed when an even more ancient man drove it away. The other two people, a couple in their forties, hadn't brought their pads and I jokingly asked them if they were saving themselves for later.

"Er, yes," said the slim, hatchet-faced man, before glancing at his wife.

"We're... beginners, you see, so we'd rather wait until Tina teaches us how... best to start," the previously serene lady stuttered in an accent not altogether unlike Angela and Malcolm's.

"Ah, did you sign up for the course quite late?" I asked, beginning to put two and two together, or rather eight and two, as I suspected that the big man had somehow inveigled them to come along to make up the numbers.

"Yes, we decided at the last minute," he said in a deep, lilting voice. "Felt like trying something new, you know."

"Ah, good. Oh, I believe there are other guests at the hotel from your part of the world," I said with a conniving smile, as I didn't care a hoot why they'd come and assumed that Malcolm had footed the bill.

He grinned. "Yes, I think the two couples we saw at breakfast are from... our part of the world."

"I believe they stumbled upon the hotel the other day," I said, resisting a strong impulse to wink, as she hadn't yet twigged that I was, or soon would be, in on the cunning ruse to bolster Angela's morale.

"Yes, one chap said they'd been passing and decided to drop in."

"For four nights," I said.

A short but significant look then passed between them and her face relaxed. He and I would probably have gone on skirting around the subject, but as the car sketcher had wandered away and the fountain sketcher was plunged in creative thought at the other end of the table, she murmured that her boss had persuaded them to come.

"Malcolm?" I mouthed.

"No, not the big boss, but he's behind it. I was offered a week off with pay, and a free holiday, so we came."

"And the other two couples?"

"The same, I think, but we're not supposed to talk to them. I think they've got the best deal, as they can go off in their hire cars, but we have to stick around and pretend to like drawing."

"It'll be fun, and we can eat and drink as much as we want," he said, before beckoning the waiter and ordering a large beer.

When I saw the church sketcher approaching I told them we could go out for a drive another day.

"We'd like that," she said.

When the company had reassembled, had another drink, and mutually admired each other's sketches, which weren't at all bad, I paid the not inconsiderable bill and went off to fetch the car. Poor, unsuspecting Angela, I thought, before wondering how many more subsidised guests Malcolm had lined up and how long he'd keep it up for. I'd ask him on Wednesday, I decided, so that he'd know what a perceptive pitch and putt partner he had.

# 22

"You don't need to be bloody Maigret to cotton on to that, Alan," Malcolm said on the third fairway when John had gone loping off after his well-driven ball. Driven, not pitched, because the big man had decided that the proper course at Monforte was a more fitting scenario for seducing the man into buying a house. He'd paid for our rounds and even hired a set of clubs for John, though I still had to share his bag.

"You should have told me about the special guests though, or I might have put my foot in it."

"You're more likely to now, as you're about as good at concealing your feelings as a whipped puppy." I flinched as he whipped a five-iron from the bag which it was still my privilege to carry. "I'd stay away from the Norfolk folk, if I were you. I do *not* want Angela to find out, understand?"

"Yes."

"How've your outings been then?"

I told him that after my first dithering attempt to entertain them, I'd subsequently played the strong, mostly silent type and that the better weather had enabled them to sketch on the mountain, which they'd enjoyed very much.

"Good. Play your ball, as the hotshot's waiting for us."

I almost made the green with a grass-cutting wallop.

"John's pretty good, isn't he?" I said.

"Yes, not much of a player my foot, but I'll put my envious feelings aside and show you how to sell a house," he said, before slicing his shot.

"Bad luck."

"I did it on purpose, you chump."

"Er, shouldn't I be the one to broach the subject of houses with him? Angela told me I ought to get some practice."

"How can I trust you not to mess up when you've forgotten my crib sheet again?"

"I didn't forget. I just haven't finished it yet," I said, as it was proving no easy task to fit everything Malcolm might need to know on a single sheet, which I was determined to do, with a view to gallantly handing them out to potential house buyers, along with my card. It had been Inma's idea, of course, but one I meant to execute to the best of my ability.

Once all our balls were on the green, Malcolm murmured that my masterclass was about to begin.

"I'm all ears," I replied, before sending a ten-yard putt to within a foot of the hole, receiving a thumbs-up sign from John for my fine effort. "Should I have played it worse?" I whispered.

"Play as well as you like, as long as he wins," he muttered. "John! I can't get used to this bloody putter," he bellowed after bobbling his ball straight past the hole.

John slid his own ball in from six feet, before approaching Malcolm and *grasping* his arm, the reckless fool. I needn't have worried, yet again, as the colossus proved to be putty in the slim man's hands and allowed himself to be moulded into an ergonomically sound putting position.

He potted the putt, or is that in snooker? Anyway, the ball went down and Malcolm thanked him effusively, seeming like an entirely different person from the one I knew. He even looked smaller as he hung onto John's every word while during the next half dozen holes he taught him not only how to drive and chip, but also to perform approach, lay-up, punch and flop shots – John's words, not mine – until by the halfway mark Malcolm's game had improved considerably.

"You haven't even mentioned houses yet," I hissed at the tenth tee.

"All in good time, lad. Can't you see what I'm up to?"

"I think so."

The trouble with golf is that when someone is imparting a non-golfing masterclass on the course, you have to try to get your ball close to theirs in order to catch it all. I believe that John eased off on his drives in order to give Malcolm something to aim at, but my ball always fell either eighty yards short or thirty yards wide, so I only got the gist of what Malcolm was saying to him, mostly on the greens.

On the eleventh hole their talk was of retirement abroad in general terms, and by the twelfth Spain had been identified as the prime destination for excellent golf and, of secondary importance, lifestyle. Little was said on the thirteenth – maybe Malcolm was superstitious – but on the fourteenth the Valencia region was featuring, more specifically Alicante by the fifteenth. Inland Alicante was outplaying the busy, expensive coastal area on the sixteenth, while the seventeenth was given over to reflection. On the eighteenth green Malcolm told him that Alan was a handy man to know if he ever considered looking into property in the lovely but inexpensive area around the hotel.

"Is that right, Alan?"

I glanced up after putting and Malcolm gave me the nod.

"Yes, I know the ins and outs of it pretty well, I suppose," I said, before crouching to adjust my laces. Would Malcolm think it a good idea for me to introduce John to Juanca, or ought I to take him in hand myself?

"Alan knows the most trustworthy estate agents around there. Don't you, Alan?"

"Oh, yes."

"And the best builders, eh, Alan?"

"Oh, yes."

"Alan helped us to buy the hotel and also found us the builder. We're ever so pleased that we met him."

"It's a fine hotel," said John. He sank his putt and shook the losers' hands. "Thanks for the game, and now let me buy you both lunch. I'd like to talk some more about houses and things."

Having been warned away from the nice Norfolk couple, I was unable to fulfil my promise of taking them out and about, but the next morning I deftly separated John and his wife Susan from the others after breakfast and whisked them away in the Toyota.

"We had a landscape class this morning," Susan murmured from the back seat.

"Yes, but Alan's going to show us some lovely landscape with houses on it, aren't you, Alan?"

"That's right," I said, trying to assess Susan's mood through the mirror. I deduced that John had been sharing his new enthusiasm for buying a house in the area with her ever since returning from our long and garrulous post-golf lunch, during which I'd eased my way into the conversation while Malcolm gradually eased his way out of it. Oh yes, I'd told him, I knew all the estate agents and all the builders within a radius of twenty miles and was in no doubt that the charming, honest Juan Carlos – using his full name in order to avoid wanker jokes – and the dour but supremely capable Cristóbal were the cream of a frankly dodgy crop. This last bit caused Malcolm to wince, due to the ambiguous nature of the statement – were they not dodgy, or just less dodgy? – but John lapped it up anyway and on our return he trotted off to tell his wife where they were going to spend their retirement.

Now, peeking into the mirror, I wasn't altogether sure that she'd bought this lifelong package deal of his, so rather than risk clamping up or, even worse, babbling myself out of a sale, I decided to drive straight to Juanca's and place them in his capable hands. I'd warned him that we'd be coming sometime in the morning, so he was hard at work in his office when we entered at half past nine.

"Ah, hola, Alan. How's it going?" he said from the desk upon which lay a plethora of papers.

"Muy bien, Juanca. Here's the delightful couple I told you about. He's as keen as mustard, but she's not sold on the idea yet," I said rapidly, in case they understood a bit of Spanish, although he'd told me they knew very little. "John, Susan, this is Juan Carlos, the man who found my sister's wonderful chalet, my partner Inma's charming cave house, and the neglected mansion which the builder Cristóbal transformed into the hotel where you're staying."

Juanca, already on his feet, appeared to float around his desk, before shaking their hands and welcoming them to the area, all the while assessing their respective states of mind, I knew. We were soon crossing the street to the bar, where the owner greeted him more effusively than usual, as did a few of the regulars who he'd persuaded to receive him joyfully whenever he entered with new foreigners. It cost him a few drinks, he'd once told me, but was worth every cent, and on this occasion it seemed to do the trick with Susan, as she smiled brightly on seeing these scenes of brotherly bonhomie.

"Are people here always so cheerful in the morning, Alan?" she asked me.

"Usually, but especially now, with so many months of warm sunshine to look forward to," I said, though most local people found the summer heat tremendously tiresome, especially those who had to work outside.

Over coffee, Juanca showed great interest in his guests, quizzing them about their stay at the hotel and not mentioning houses until John brought up the subject.

"We wouldn't mind seeing a few chalets with pools," he said.

"Yes, we can do that, today or another day," Juanca said airily, before asking them how the drawing and painting was going.

Susan told him it was going fine, while John nodded obediently.

"Well, I don't want to keep you from your course, but I could quickly show you a few places and then take you back to the hotel, if you like."

This I understood to mean that my presence wasn't required, which I didn't mind, as although they were a pleasant couple, I hadn't bonded with them especially strongly and I could see that Juanca knew that he'd have to work his magic on Susan, John already being hooked on the idea, thanks mostly to Malcolm. While crossing the road I quietly asked Juanca if the Frenchman had chosen his unfinished chalet yet.

"Almost. One that was scarcely begun. Good news for my cousin, and for us. You can go now," he murmured, before ushering them into his Audi.

"Are you not coming, Alan?" Susan asked cheerfully.

"I'd like to, but I'd better get back to the hotel."

"OK," she said, before shutting the passenger door, Juanca having positioned his prey by his side.

Pleased by my morning's work, I drove back to the hotel and on spotting Tina and her students down by the pine trees I found myself climbing into my Clio. It was Inma's midweek day off, after all, and if I stayed there was a danger that the Norfolk couple might collar me and ask me to fulfil my promise of taking them out. Malcolm had ordered me to stay away from them, so, as Jesús might have said, what could I do? The fact that Angela might have liked me to stick around did cross my mind, but the prospect of seeing that smug so-and-so Gerardo tipped the balance, so I sneaked off down the drive, feeling very much like a truant.

"I feel like a truant," I told Inma when I got home and joined her on the patio.

"Yes, it's naughty of you really."

I filled her in on my house sale prospects.

"Hmm, the Frenchman sounds promising, but the English couple, well, that might take more time."

I leaned back in Zefe's former outdoor chair and stretched luxuriantly. "Ah, I've got all the time in the world."

"But not long as a free man, I'm afraid."

"No?"

"Unless you change your mind about marrying me, because the date is set for Saturday the 26th, courtesy of Rosa's uncle."

I sat bolt upright. "Ooh, so we'll have to start organising things and… things."

She patted the whitening knuckles of my right hand. "Relax, you don't have to do anything."

"Nothing at all?"

"No, I prefer to arrange things myself, though it'll be a very simple affair."

I sighed, "Story of my life, doing nothing at all. I sell houses without doing anything, and now I'm marrying the most beautiful woman for miles around without lifting a finger."

"Ah, speaking of fingers, that is the one thing I want you to do, buy the wedding bands. I'll give you an old ring of mine to take to the jeweller's, so you just have to ask for two plain gold bands. Will you be able to manage that?"

My brow creased in thought.

"It's not difficult, Alan."

"I know, but I'm thinking about what to have engraved on them; inside them, I mean."

"Oh, nothing corny, please."

"No, but we must have something. I'll give it some thought and go tomorrow."

"Why not give it some thought while you work on your little allotment? There are lots of weeds already."

"Ah, yes, I'd forgotten about that." I stood up and kissed her on the forehead. "I'll do it now, as time and weeds wait for no man."

So it was that the rest of the day was spent weeding, thinking about inscriptions, and finishing Malcolm's crib sheet. The following morning the jeweller dismissed most of my ideas as being too long and, quite frankly, corny, so I settled for *semper amemus*, the Latin phrase for *Let us love forever*, which I liked because it's similar in Spanish and in the best possible taste. It rained in the afternoon, so I saw little point in going to the hotel, but on Saturday I decided I'd better put in an appearance, it being the last full day of the course. I didn't fancy descending on them at breakfast, so I got there at about ten and found Gerardo in his customary spot behind the reception desk.

"Buenos días, Gerardo," I enunciated clearly, intending to mince no more words with the blighter.

"Hello, Alan. Angela has been wondering where you've been," he said with slyly narrowed eyes.

"Hmm, dónde está?"

"She's out, with some of the students, in the Toyota," he said, savouring every word, the hound.

"Ah, y dónde está Malcolm?"

"Playing golf, with the student called John."

Damn, I should have called him, but then again he could have called me, I thought.

"You look worried, Alan," he said, grinning like a hyena.

I tutted and leant on the counter. "Yo? No, no."

"Perhaps you ought to be worried, as the driver and supposed entertainer of the guests doesn't normally disappear for three days."

"Dos," I said, exhibiting two fingers in the way us Brits send folk like him to the devil. Having worked in England, he understood the sentiment.

"If you were a member of my staff, you would be sacked." He shrugged and picked a bit of fluff from his jacket. "However, it's up to Angela to decide what to do with you."

By way of reply I grasped his greasy hair and dragged him right over the counter, before swinging him round like an Olympic hammer and flinging him straight through the window, in my imagination at least, but after visualising that pleasant occurrence I settled for saying the following, in Spanish, as always.

"Gerardo." I cleared my throat and folded my arms. "Gerardo, it is no business of yours what I do with my time. Unlike you, I am a free agent and do as I please. While you are… chained to this hotel, day after day, I am busy doing deals and making money, just like that." I clicked my fingers. "Some of us are slaves to one employer, while others use our initiative and make our way in the world as free men."

He glowered and gripped the counter.

I placed my hands on my hips, puffed out my chest, raised myself to my full height, and smiled indulgently. "This, Gerardo, is the way of the world. Some are born to serve, others to… triumph," I said, my well of inspiration running dry.

"I shall tell Angela this. She'll be interested to hear your opinions," he growled.

"Ha." I casually swatted the air, before pointing at the open door. "I shall go, Gerardo, to enjoy the warm spring breeze. Now you may get on with your work."

I'd taken two or three dignified steps toward the door when he began to speak, in *Spanish*.

"You damn guiris are all the same. You're all useless sons of bitches and you only succeed in Spain if you have money behind you. You, Alan, are more pathetic than most. Always smiling and prattling, but without a gram of common sense in your head. I wouldn't give you a job cleaning the bloody toilets. Even that gypsy swine is more competent than you, you great gangling waste of space," he said, or words very much to that effect.

Slightly shaken by this outburst, my nostrils quivered like those of a bull about to charge, and charge I did, metaphorically speaking.

"Gerardo, my friend," I began in *English*, truth always being stranger than fiction. "If I tell Angela what you've just said you'll lose this job, just like you lost the one in Preston, eh? Eh? EH!?" I cried, my 'ehs' ascending in volume as indicated.

He gulped, and I know a good gulp when I see one, before hanging his head and shuffling something on the desk behind the counter.

"You messed up badly in Preston, didn't you?" I said, in Spanish once more.

Shuffle, shuffle.

"Steal money, did you? Or was it something worse?"

Shuffle, sniff, shuffle, sniff.

If there's one thing I hate it's seeing a grown man cry, even one like Gerardo, and if truth be told I felt that I'd gone a bit far. Having hardly argued with anyone for years, I'd become bitter and vengeful all too easily, and if I could have wound back the clock I'd have taken back... no, would I heck, as he deserved every word of it, the snivelling toad, but the jibe about Preston had been a bit below the belt. Feeling almost certain that he wasn't a dangerous sexual predator, and given the fact that if anyone could make a success of the isolated hotel it was him, I then apologised for my outburst and told him that it might be best to keep our little chat to ourselves.

"Yes, Alan, I think that would be best," he said in Spanish, so I'd scored a victory of sorts, but one that was to cause me no elation.

"Good, I'm glad."

"I also apologise for my outburst. You're a nice man and so is Arturo. I got angry, that's all."

"Me too."

He wiped his nose with his silky hankie. "And I work so hard to make this place a success."

"I know you do. Let's shake hands and put this stupid incident behind us."

"All right, Alan."

We'd just softly shaken hands when the Toyota pulled up outside, and to Gerardo's credit he exhibited no pleasure at the prospect of the grilling I was probably about to receive from Angela. He winked and smiled complicitly, in fact, before sitting down at the computer and smoothing his hair into place. I strode boldly outside and greeted them all cheerfully, receiving friendly replies from the students and a wry smile from Angela.

"I was a bit late today," I said when they'd gone inside.

She locked the Toyota and pocketed the keys. "Today?"

"Er, yes, well, I've been rather busy," I said, bowing my head *à la Gerardo*.

She chuckled. "This first course must have flown by for you, Alan."

"Yes, it's… yes. I… er, don't want you to pay me for the little that I've done."

"As you wish. I think this week might prove quite profitable for you anyway," she said as Gerardo's BMW slowed to a halt with a grinning Malcolm at the wheel and a beaming John by his side.

She chuckled again. "Go and see how the land lies."

I obeyed.

"Good game, John?"

"Great, thanks. I played a decent round and Malc's game is really coming along. We're off with Juan Carlos again this afternoon. Susan's slowly coming around to my way of thinking."

"Take your time and have a good think about things when you get home," I said sagely and, I believed, astutely, though Malcolm's brief examination of the clouds suggested that he thought otherwise.

"Have you done my crib sheet yet?"

I smiled, my quarrel with Gerardo now a fading memory. "Of course, hang on." I dashed to the car and during my flight my mind worked at such lightning speed that when I returned I gave the sheet not to Malcolm, Malc to his pals, but to John.

"I made this for him, but I can soon print another. It's just a few pointers to get you going."

"Cheers, Alan. We're both ready to get stuck into some Spanish."

I felt like patting his head, but instead shook his hand, before turning to the big man.

"I'll print you anoth–"

"Pitch and putt on Monday. I'll pick you up at eight in your Toyota."

"Oh, yes, we'd better change the name."

"After golf. Come on, John, I'll show you where I plan to make my mini pitch and putt, all being well."

Left alone, I left, sensing that my days as a tour guide were over.

# 23

The build-up to the wedding was strange in the sense that there didn't appear to be any build-up at all. Having soon collected the two correctly sized and inscribed rings, one evening I asked Inma if she was sure there wasn't anything else I could do.

"No, dear, it's all under control."

"But you don't seem to be doing much either."

"There's little to do."

"Who's coming?"

"My parents, Natalia, Cathy and Bernie."

"Is that all?"

"Alan, we said we wanted a quiet affair. If you invite one person, you have to invite another, and so it goes on."

"What about the rest of your family?"

"Oh, we'll arrange a lunch or something in Murcia sometime."

"Then maybe I'll arrange a lunch or something for the folk here sometime."

"You do that."

"What about a honeymoon?"

She tutted softly. "Later. I can't possibly get away from the bar just now, not unless we get another cook right away, and even if we do, I'd rather go in June when it's warmer."

"OK."

"There is one thing I want you to do before the wedding though."

"Your wish is my command, dear."

"I want you to sleep at Cathy and Bernie's the night before."

"What for?"

"It's tradition, of course. My parents will come here on Friday night and my mother won't want you hanging around."

"All right," I said, quite fancying an evening with Bern so soon before tying the knot, and with Cathy too, of course. "I'm going to buy a new jacket, trousers, shirt and tie," I declared.

"Good idea. I've seen a dress I might buy."

"A white one?"

"Of course not. I'm a forty-five-year-old mother."

"Natalia could be a bridesmaid."

She laughed. "That'll be the day."

"How is she?"

"Fine, studying hard. Did you hear what I said about our cook?"

"Er, no."

"Randi's gone."

"Ah," I said, my mind still full of wedding-related thoughts.

She tutted. "Did you hear what I said?"

"Yes. Has she got another job or something?"

"No, she's gone, as in left home. She didn't come into work this morning and called later to say that she'd left Arvid and gone off with Jaime."

"Who's Jaime?" I asked, beginning to sense that something was amiss.

"The military man."

"Ah, so she hasn't gone far then."

"Oh, I don't know. Juan Antonio suspects that they've left the area."

"Where does he think they've gone?" I said, my curiosity finally aroused.

She slapped the table. "I don't know and I refuse to take part in gossipy speculation about this. She's let us down and quite frankly she's let herself down too. One oughtn't to act in this irresponsible way. If she wants to be with this man, she should go about things in the right way, instead of running off like a giddy girl."

"All right, love. Not another word," I said, surprised by her vehement response, which wasn't like her at all.

She sighed. "I'm sure we'll find out soon enough anyway."

"Poor Arvid. Do you know how he... never mind, I was going to pop over to my sister's tomorrow anyway."

At just after eleven the next morning I rolled to a halt after a pleasant bike ride in the warm sunshine. On spotting me, Bernie jumped down from Spartacus and loped across his impeccable field of olive saplings, peeling off his tractor gloves.

"I'm gradually building up a picture of recent events," he said, slightly breathless.

"Morning, Bernie."

"Morning. So, Randi hopped it yesterday morning after Arvid went out on his bike. At first she went to the randy soldier's house, but when Arvid got back and found her gone, he went to confront them and there was a shoot-out."

"A what?"

"You know, gunfire. It's at this point that opinions begin to differ, and I've had a hell of a time finding out, because Inma and Rosa glare at anyone who they think are gossiping about it."

"Just wind back to the gunfire bit, Bern."

He took a few deep breaths. "Well, old Juan Antonio insists that a single shot was heard and that about an hour later Randi and the man were seen driving through the village, heading north.

Other folk say there was a proper gunfight and Arvid was killed, but that's nonsense, because I've seen him at home this morning, through the binoculars. It's all very amusing really."

"What was Arvid doing?"

"Shooting his biathlon rifle at them, we think."

"No, I mean this morning."

"Setting off on his bike."

"Then he can't be wounded, or very affected by it all."

"And the other two must be all right, unless they were bleeding to death in the car, ha ha."

"You're taking this very lightly, Bernie. Has anyone been round to the man's house to look?"

"I don't know. I think they're all too busy whispering about it in the bar to bother."

"Have you finished here?"

"Can't you see that I've got two more rows to go?"

"The whole field looks ploughed to me."

"No, two rows to go. Ploughing brings the moisture up. Jesús taught me that."

"Hmm. Look, I'll ride over to have a look at the scene of the supposed shoot-out, then I'll meet you back at the house."

After establishing the exact location of the House of Sin, I rode the two or three kilometres along the tracks and found a chalet not unlike Cathy and Bernie's, but with less land and more weeds pushing through the gravel. I located a floppy part of the metal fence and climbed over, before slowly circling the house. At first I didn't find any evidence of shooting, but on closer inspection I spotted a small hole in the upper left-hand corner of a front window, the glass slightly fragmented around it. Arvid hadn't shot to kill then, as he was a master marksman and must have chosen his spot, intending, I deduced, to make it clear that he didn't take kindly to them shacking up in the neighbourhood. After another tour round in search of further bullet holes – there were none – I clambered over the fence and headed off, pleased with my detective work but worried that Arvid might soon be in the hands of the law.

Over a glass of lemon tea I told Bernie of my findings and fears.

"Hmm, if they'd rung the cops they'd have come for him already. I know a lot of people have guns here, but I think it's still a crime to fire them at folk."

"At the corner of a window, but still." I looked through the binoculars and saw their small car. "Maybe we should go round if he comes back."

"He's normally out for hours on the bike."

"Maybe you should go round later then."

"Nah, he knows where we are. He might think Randi's sent me and blow my head off."

"I doubt it. Where's Cathy?"

"In town, seeing an oldie then shopping."

"What does she think about all this?"

"Not a lot. Says she could see it coming and didn't believe the bit about the shooting. Come on, I'll show you the plot."

As he'd predicted, things were really growing fast in the spring sunshine and I was proud to tell him that my little plot was weed-free.

"Unfortunately it might be tomato-free too, as I was lost in thought when I was weeding. Thinking about the wedding, you know," I said, examining his face for signs of secret preparations.

"When is it again?"

"The 26th."

"Ah, yes."

"Has Cathy not mentioned it?"

"Not much. I think we're coming here for a bit of lunch afterwards, but I'm not sure. What's up?" he said on observing my wrinkling nose.

"Oh, I don't know. I mean, we've agreed to make it a really quiet affair and maybe invite folk to lunch another day, but… well, I've never been married before, and the closer it gets, the more I think I wouldn't mind a bit of pomp and… you know."

"If you want that you should become a Catholic then. You'd have to have instruction and then be received into the church and all that, although as Inma's divorced, the priest might not want to wed you. No, heathens like you ought to just sign your names and have done with it."

"You're a heathen and you had a great wedding."

"Ah, well, the C of E isn't too fussy about religion anymore."

I sighed and spied on Arvid's place again. There was no sign of him, so I cycled home, not wishing to provoke Inma's wrath by getting gossiped at in the bar.

When she arrived home I did tell her about the hole in the window.

"A warning shot, I think," she said with an air of finality, so the subject was shelved for the time being.

On the day that Inma drove to Alicante to sign her divorce papers, Juanca called to tell me that the Frenchman had bought a partially built chalet for the modest sum of €57,000.

"Great."

"Yes, it's not much for us, but Cristóbal's drawing up plans for his architect to sign as we speak, and it seems fairly certain that he'll do the work, so that will be a much better payday for us."

"Great, and the English couple?"

"John and Susan? Well, they took the advice some imbecile gave them and went home to think about it, didn't they?"

"Er, yes, I believe so," I said, hanging my head, despite being on the phone.

"Well, they're coming out again soon and I think they'll buy, so you didn't mess up after all."

My head rose with a jerk and I beamed. "Yes, I was sure it was the best tactic. It isn't always good to rush people. I could see they weren't the type for that."

"Hmm."

"Are you doing anything this weekend?" I asked, wondering if Inma might be planning to surprise me by inviting people on the sly, even him.

"Me? The usual. Working on Saturday and sitting in my lonely flat on Sunday. Why do you ask?"

"Oh, no reason, but try to get out and do some exercise. You'll feel better for it."

"Yes, well, I might walk to the bar for a beer. Find me some more buyers, Alan."

"I'll try."

By then I was calling Beth every week, and although she'd given my card to a few people, my next victim had yet to call me. I say victim, but the truth was that my previous scruples about flogging houses seemed to have disappeared. The Frenchman, who I'd met only once, had got a bargain, and I sincerely thought that Spain was the right choice for John and Susan, as they were eager to leave their increasingly crowded Northamptonshire town and they both hated cold, rainy weather. He'd even emailed me to say that they were taking Spanish classes, which pleased me a lot, as you know my feelings about learning the language. All in all I was happy with my lot, and Malcolm had promised to tell me if Angela wished me to do any specific tasks at the hotel, as I still felt that I owed her one after my dismal attempt to play a part I was eminently unsuited for. During our last game of pitch and putt he'd told me that a trickle of genuine guests had begun to stay and that for the moment he was holding the 'extra' guests he had lined up in reserve, which was good news indeed.

Juan expected to be doing some driving for the furniture company soon, as the ex-jailbird had decided to go it alone – driving, not committing fraud – so I'd tag along with him on his trips, though he had no plans to repeat the onerous drive to Vitoria. Northwards Inma and I would certainly head, however, as we were already planning a belated honeymoon to Asturias and Cantabria in early summer, and we'd head up north with Cathy and Bernie another time too. I'd bought a William IV gold half sovereign as a pre-wedding gift to us both and would put the rest of the contents of the cornflakes box in our soon-to-be-opened joint account, so I really couldn't have been happier.

# 24

"I really couldn't be happier," I told Cathy and Bernie as he parked their Ford Focus near the town hall.

We climbed out and Cathy adjusted the white rose in the buttonhole of my new blue jacket, before straightening the silk tie that Bernie had tied for me. There wasn't a soul outside the town hall and I suggesting going inside to find the office where we were to be unceremoniously hitched.

"No, let's hang about here till they arrive," Cathy said.

For the next ten minutes I felt that we made a strangely overdressed trio as the townsfolk went about their business, but when Letizia came whirring around the corner, tastefully adorned with a couple of small bunches of flowers and piloted by Inma's father, my heart leapt, as there was Inma, soon stepping out in an off-the-shoulder, peach-coloured dress which showed off her delectable curves marvellously. Natalia being Natalia, she was wearing a black dress to celebrate the fateful day, but it fit her like a glove and brought out her femininity like never before, despite her new, strangely jagged haircut. I stood there beaming and waving, until Inma's mother shooed me inside, where a young chap led us into a function room, probably the council chamber. With only seven of us to occupy the twenty or so seats, the low-key nature of the ceremony struck me again, but when an older, better-dressed fellow began to officiate I concentrated on his solemn words and we were soon slipping the tasteful rings onto each other's fingers. We kissed quickly, then slightly more languorously in the corridor, before I escorted her to the 2CV and helped her into the back seat. Bernie and Natalia hopped into the front and we were soon whirring through the streets.

"That went very quickly," I murmured to Inma as we sat with our fingers entwined.

"A mere formality," she said, before kissing my cheek. "We were already man and wife."

"Yes, we were. Where to now, Bern?"

"Back to ours. I think Cathy's cooked a pie or something."

"Right. Ha, have we any champagne?"

"Some cava, I think."

"I'll never get married," said Natalia, who I then noticed was wearing make-up, something previously scorned by her. "I'll never belong to any man."

"Your mother doesn't exactly belong to me."

"Just watch him, Mamá. Don't let him boss you about."

"I won't, dear."

"Fat chance," Bernie murmured in English.

As we whirred along past fields of green fruit trees, I felt happy and hardly bothered at all by the fact that the most important event of my life was to be celebrated around their table, but when he turned into the hamlet rather than up the track, I had an inkling that a surprise was in store for me.

"Oh, look, they've found out about it," Inma said as we approached the bar, from which many familiar faces began to emerge. There was Rosa and her family, old Juan Antonio, Juan, Jesús, Arturo with a little girl, Malcolm and Angela, Álvaro, Zefe waving his stick, Cristóbal, Juanca with a youngish woman, Beth with a strapping chap, and a couple of ladies I didn't know who turned out to be old friends of Inma.

"I knew you'd do this," I said, my spine tingling from top to bottom.

"Just a few friends. We're going to celebrate with the Murcia contingent next Sunday. Come on, escort me inside."

We then walked a raucous gauntlet and suffered rice to be thrown at us, as is the tradition in Spain, before entering the bar to find it decorated with flowers and strips of satiny stuff. Most of the tables were pushed together to make a long one, in the middle of one side of which we were invited to sit.

Wonderful smells emanated from the kitchen and I asked Inma who had done the cooking.

"Our new cook, a youngster from Fortuna. He isn't quite as good as Randi, but he's keen to learn."

"Shame about Randi. She'd have enjoyed this."

"One makes one's choices. Bernie went to invite Arvid, but he didn't want to come."

"No problems with the police then?"

"No. Look, Zefe's already collared Juan Antonio, poor man."

"They're as talkative as each other. Who's that pretty woman with Juanca?"

"His new girlfriend, I think."

"What an old scamp, after his sob stories. Look, Juan and Jesús have sat down together."

"Yes, but why is Jesús prodding Malcolm?"

"Uh-oh, he won't like that."

Malcolm just took Jesús's wrist and placed it gently by his knives, as he couldn't have understood a word of his cautionary advice anyway, because a mere crib sheet works no miracles.

"Look at Arturo's lovely daughter," Inma said.

"Yes, little Rocío. I wonder if she's half-gypsy, quarter-gypsy or what? I'll have to ask him. Look at *your* lovely daughter, already annoying Cristóbal with her chatter."

"He's smiling though." She frowned. "Where's his wife?"

"Indoors, I expect. Oh, is Natalia still set on working at the hotel?"

"No, she's talking about travelling this summer now."

"Good." I scanned the table. "I must talk to Beth and her husband afterwards. They don't know anyone and I want them to have a good time."

"Yes, you should."

This made me think about money and I told Inma that I wouldn't let her father sell his lovely coin to pay for the lavish spread we were about to tuck into.

"He's already paid Rosa, but hasn't sold the coin. Don't offend him."

"I won't. This is nice, isn't it?"

"It's just right."

Inma then began our first meal together as man and wife by peeling a prawn for me.

"Ah, thank you, dear. Is this a sign of things to come?"

"No, love, I'm just showing you how not to make a mess of it. Our marriage is going to be one of equals."

"How can it be a marriage of equals when you're so much more beautiful, charming and accomplished than me?"

She popped the prawn into my mouth to shut me up.

# AFTERWORD

It's been a good while since I was a reluctant expat, which is why the series has now come to an end, but I do plan to write more in the future, as I've enjoyed penning this rambling account. For now I'll give the old fingertips a rest, but before the year is out I may well be able to offer my patient readers something new. As well as continuing my story, which I hope to do unless married life proves to be too blissfully mundane to write about, I also have a novel in the pipeline, a work begun during my previous life and not about Spain at all, but I'll have to see if I think it worth inflicting on the public when I finish it.

So, farewell for now, and thank you for reading my books.

All the best,
Alan Laycock

Printed in Great Britain
by Amazon